# Stone Roses

Editor: **Mike Evans**
Assistant Editor: **Karen O'Grady**
Production Controller: **Mark Walker**
Picture Research: **Maria Gibbs**
Art Editor: **Leigh Jones**
Design: **Ian Loats, Design Revolution**

First published in 1996 by
Hamlyn, an imprint of
Reed Consumer Books Limited,
Michelin House, 81 Fulham Road,
London SW3 6RB
and Auckland, Melbourne, Singapore and Toronto

Printed and bound in Spain.

**Picture Acknowledgements**

**All Action** /A. Phillips 54 -55, /Joel Phillips 79, /Justin
Thomas 7 right, 8 top, 29 below, 60 left, 76, 78 left,
78 below.
**Redferns** /Simon Ritter 60-61, 61.
**Retna** /Steve Double 31, /Tim Jarvis 47 top right,
/Johnny Rozsa 10, 23, /Ed Sirrs 11, /Paul Slattery 14-15,
16-17, 28 right, 37, 44, 48, 62, 63.
**S.I.N** /Peter Anderson 9, /Marina Chavez 3, /Joe Dilworth
28 left, 29 left, 29 right, /Martyn Goodacre 59, 66 left, 66
right, 72, 73 top, /Hayley Madden 4, 80, /Ed Sirrs 5, 25,
/Martyn Goodacre 65 top, /Ian T.Tilton 12 left, 58.
**Pennie Smith** 22, 27, 45, 49, 50, 51, 64-65, 65 below,
67, 68-69, 69, 70, 73 below, 74-75, 75, 77.
**Ian T. Tilton** 6 right, 6 left, 7 top, 8 below, 12 right, 13
left, 13 right, 19 , 20-21, 24 , 26, 30, 32-33, 34, 35,
36, 38, 39, 40-41, 42, 43, 46-47, 46 top left, 52-53, 54
inset top, 55 below, 56-57, 57 right, 71 below.

# Stone Roses

DAVE SIMPSON

HAMLYN

# CONTENTS

# The Best Band on the Planet

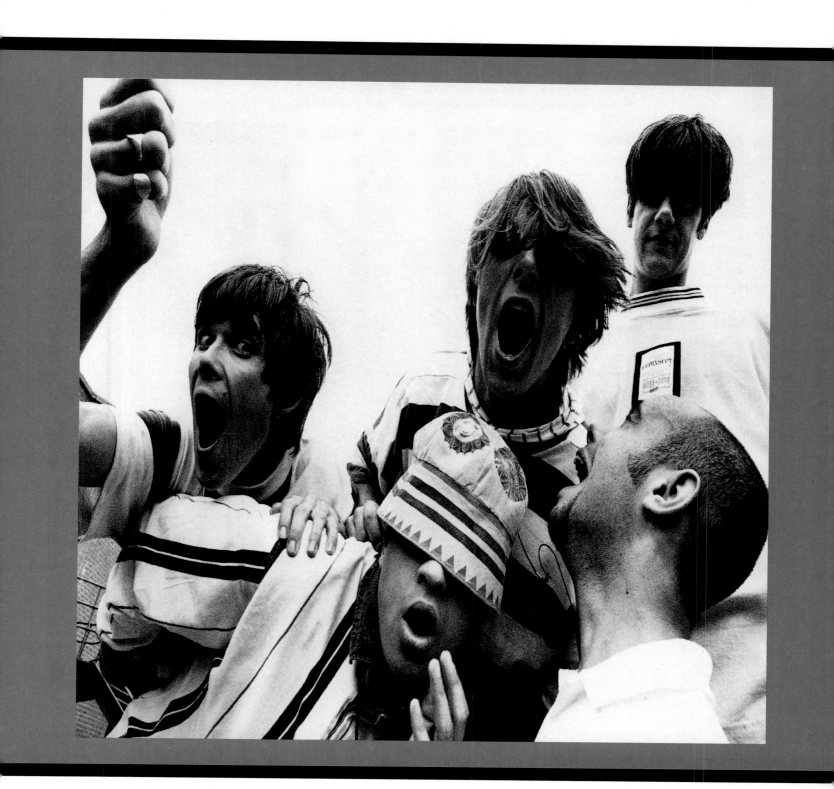

atmosphere in Leeds Warehouse on their breakthrough tour of spring '89. Maybe it was because the Leeds nightclub was half-filled with Mancunians or May's premature heat or, more likely, it was something to do with history being made. When the four brash young urchins came onstage without introduction and launched into 'Elephant Stone', nobody present had heard anything like it. Was it funk, was it dance, was it rock? And such strange words, balancing the desire of perfect love with the vitriol of purest hatred. '*I don't have to sell my soul/He's already in me*' sang Ian Brown.

## THE BEST BAND ON THE PLANET

'*WE want to be the best of everything. To be all things to all people at all times. Aim for the stars and you're gonna hit the ceiling. Never put up with second best.*' – Ian Brown, The Stone Roses

WHEN Ian Brown and John Squire were teenagers, they'd meet up with their mates on motor scooters and head for the seaside. 'It felt,' remembers John Squire, 'like we were taking over the town.'

Not long afterwards they did the same with pop. Twice. In 1989, Brown and Squire's band The Stone Roses became easily the most exciting thing to happen to British pop music in years. Back then, I was one of the many who saw the band's concerts and underwent a life-changing experience. 'The Best Band On The Planet', I called them on the front cover of my then fanzine, *Avanti!* and if anything it was an understatement. The pop universe had simply never seen anything like The Stone Roses. Their driven, euphoric pop-rock and effortless Mancunian cool captured the eyes, ears and imagination of a generation for whom the heart-racing beats of club culture slotted perfectly next to the Roses' hallucinogenic melodies and pulsating funk grooves. Oh, and on a separate level, the fashion world was certainly not prepared for the Roses – ahem – distinctive clobber, based around floppy hats, levitating fringes and improbable 22-inch flares. Well, nobody's perfect.

I can still remember the uncanny

John Squire (left) at Glasgow Green, and Mani at Blackpool's Empress Ballroom

SIX

Was the spiky mop-topped singer some angel/devil, a talented new Jagger for a modern generation, or just some absurdly charismatic estate kid with ideas above his station? Whatever, by the middle of the set, people were dancing on the tables. The party had just begun.

Six weeks later, 'She Bangs The Drums' was in the charts and The Stone Roses had begun their first ascent into pop legend. Their debut, eponymous LP is regarded by many as the best of the Eighties. It was certainly the most significant. Overnight, The Stone Roses had achieved something that happens maybe once every ten years. They created – rather than captured – the zeitgeist of their time. Along with Happy Mondays, they crafted a soundtrack for a new generation, but the Roses were the first to break. Their music may have had very slight echoes of Manchester's past (the Martin Hannett-y intro to 'Adored', the revolving ACR drumbeat appropriated for 'Resurrection'), but it was fed through the insurgent House boom, The Byrds, and quietly creative guitarist John Squire's studio trickery. Together with the band's naughty boy next door image and their instantly memorable choruses, 'The Stone Roses' marked the unification of rock music with the Ecstacy-fuelled dance rhythms that were already starting to dominate youth culture. Added to that was the band's relentless self-belief, which bordered on arrogance but was undoubtedly justified. In the face of bloated

Drummer 'Reni' Wren (inset) and Ian Brown on bongos

stadium excesses and tawdry, navel-gazing 'alternative' mediocrities, the Roses came along and kicked the whole music scene into action. Overnight they managed to restore ambition to rock.

The repercussions were instantaneous and far-reaching. Kids wanted to be in bands again, and since then the Roses' sound has proved the basis for the careers of many of today's successes, such as The Bluetones, The Charlatans, Shed Seven, Puressence and, not least, fellow Mancunians Oasis, whose belligerent melodiousness owes as much to the Roses music and attitude as it does to The Beatles.

Meanwhile, the Roses themselves have moved on. Blighted by managerial and record company disputes and, for a time, prevented from recording by crippling litigation, the Roses re-emerged at the end of '94 with the brilliantly self-explanatory 'Second Coming', an album that reached far into rock guitar history and the darker recesses of the human condition and reflected the mood of the band and their time as accurately as its predecessor. Suddenly,

The Stone Roses were again the band of the moment. 'Second Coming' also demonstrated that, five years after the rhetoric of their emergence, they could still zoom into the the Top Five. Although, this time around, the only flares were the dazzling pyrotechnics unleashed by John Squire's immaculate electrified guitar. Thank God !

'Second Coming' deservedly went platinum and affirmed that The Stone Roses are, if nothing, survivors. In 1995 they had all this to prove again following the mysterious departure of cornerstone drummer Reni. But with the addition of sticksman Robbie Jay Maddix the band showed that they must evolve and, what's more, they could still cut it as a live act. The comeback U.K. tour in December 1995 sold out in less than 24 hours, with many of the gigs provoking hysterical, religious scenes.

But in 1996 The Stone Roses face their toughest test yet with the exit of guitarist and songwriter John Squire. In rock history terms, his departure is at least as significant as the disappearance of Richey Edwards from The Manic Street Preachers in 1995 or

the exit of Peter Gabriel from Genesis, 20 years earlier. Those bands have survived and, indeed, prospered, and whilst the future of The Stone Roses remains slightly shaky and uncertain, it is unlikely that Squire's departure is the end of the story.

Here, then, is the beginning...

**Brixton Academy, December '95**

★★★★★★★★★★★★★★★★★

# Sowing the Seeds

## BECAUSE YOU'RE YOUNG

THEIR two albums span two decades, but the history of The Stone Roses in fact covers four. Around the time Beach Boy Brian Wilson retreated into a sandpit complete with his piano, John Squire (28.11.62, Sagittarius) first met Ian Brown (20.2.63, Pisces) in a similar sand-filled box, sometime in 1967. Then, as now, the duo were polar opposites: Squire was shy and almost painfully withdrawn, Brown tough, popular and confident. But the original bond at the heart of the group was formed, although it would be many years later that the pair would unite within music.

The pair lived two doors apart on Sylvan Avenue (oddly enough the home of another Mancunian phenomenon, The Bee Gees, two decades earlier) in Sale, a satellite town just south of Greater Manchester. The future Roses were outsiders from the start. Born to working class backgrounds around Manchester (Ian's father was a joiner, John's worked for GEC), they turned their backs on conventional lifestyles early on. At school, John Squire was the quietest boy in the class, his head in a solitary world of crayons and drawings.

'I was good at art,' he told me in 1995. 'I drew cartoons of the teachers. There was this attitude that it didn't matter. The art teacher had that Bohemian "I can't get the funds so why should I bother attitude."

Ian Brown and John Squire form The Patrol . . . childhoods and scooter-riding days . . . Ian's journey around Europe . . . the Northern Soul all-nighters . . . The Patrol become English Rose . . . concerts in Sweden . . . enter Reni . . . working with Martin Hannett . . . and finding the manager . . .

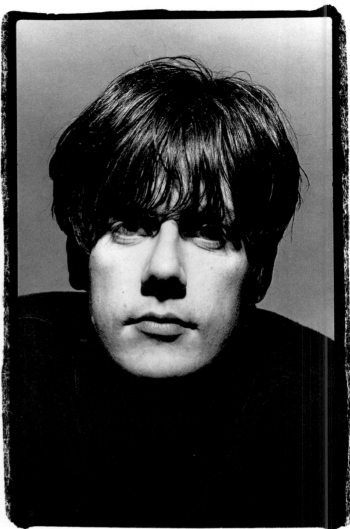

**Ian Brown (left) and John Squire in August 1989**

and the class saw art as time off. We only studied for two years. I ended up dropping games so I could do more.'

Tellingly, John Squire wasn't so much spurred on by his peers' lack of interest as his own inwardly held ambitions. As he puts it now, 'I always had that drive.'

At home, John's life would vibrate to the sounds of Elvis, The Beatles and Peggy Lee. John has known Ian Brown almost as long as he can remember.

'I've vague memories of meeting him at his friend's house,' Squire recalled recently. 'It was like an arranged marriage, a parental thing. The school catchment area had a line that went down the street. He was on one side, I was on the other, but eventually we went to the same secondary school. I didn't

really get to know him until punk. He was somebody locally who was into the same music. We'd swap records and things.'

They bonded over punk. 'At the time, it felt like an illicit underworld,' said John.

## TEENAGE WILDLIFE
SQUIRE was definatley the more 'dogmatic' of the two, being a fan of rebel rockers The Clash (he liked their painted trousers best) whereas Brown's musical preference leaned towards groups such as The Stranglers and The Jam. Ian was much rowdier, not quite one of the lads but...

'It was definitely a case of opposites attract,' remembered John, in my *I-D* interview. 'He had records I didn't. He was more popular, yeah. I was happy to be a

loner. I prefer it. We hung about for a short period, then when we started the band it became more permanent.'

Gary 'Mani' Mounfield (16.11.62, Scorpio) was following a similar trajectory out of school and into punk and Northern Soul. He'd been in a band with John already (The Mill) but they hadn't gigged.

When Mani met Ian...

'There were some National Front skinheads in North Manchester who'd been shakin' a lot of me mates up,' recalled Mounfield. 'So Ian Brown and a crew of his mates from South Manchester met up with us through a mutual friend and we went and dealt with 'em. We've been mates ever since.'

This anecdote says everything about Brown. He was already extremely street

**Gary 'Mani' Mounfield and Reni, August 1989**

tough and principled, with plenty of the burning idealism that would crop up later on in songs like 'Waterfall', 'Sugar Spun Sister', 'Resurrection' and 'How Do You Sleep': songs brimming with themes of betrayal, revenge, justice and insurrection. The later-to-be-songwriting partnership with Squire was – back then – consummated on a motor scooter.

'A Lambretta was a very desirable object,' explained John, again in my late '95 interview for *I-D* magazine. 'Ian wanted one. I got one. Did it up, painted it. I wanted to show it off to other people who liked scooters.'

Looking back, John Squire now describes his state of mind at this time as being 'Progressive. Never satisfied with where I am or what I'd done.'

Meanwhile, Ian Brown was developing similarly itchy feet, hitch-hiking his way around Europe in a rite of passage that would later form the basis of the classic single, 'Made Of Stone'.

'I've always been on the move,' Brown told *Sounds* in 1989. 'When I lived in Sale I never hung about there. I hung about with lads all over the city. I've been to every seaside resort in England and most cities. I've been to most of Europe just moving about. It's what I'm into doing.'

As a teenager, Brown's hunger for experience was matched by an equally strong desire to avoid the fates that awaited most of his contemporaries. Well, could you really imagine that spiky moptop flopping over a suit?!

'I never wanted to work on a building site or go to university,' Ian told me once. 'I didn't think what I was going to do. I just drifted. I'm still drifting.

'The first thing I did was scrub pots,' he told *NME*. 'Been left school two days and I'm in this big oven in a hotel with the chef kicking me. That's when I realised I didn't want a job. I stood it about three weeks.'

John Squire's employment history makes for an equally disastrous CV.

'I worked at Cosgrove Hall, makers of 'Dangermouse',' he revealed in *NME* in 1989. 'I wasn't working as an illustrator . I was in the Mud Pie Dept.'

Clearly, all was not sweetness and light for the lads at this point in their lives. And so uderstandably, they formed a pop group.

## FACING THE MUSIC

ACCORDING to the few who can remember seeing them, The Patrol were 'orrible: far too Clash influenced and not a band to let tunes get in the way of a row. Lining up Brown (on bass, curiously), Squire (inevitably, on lead guitar), Andy Cousens (vocals guitar) and Simon Wolstencroft (now of The Fall, on drums), The Patrol spent 1980 and '81 playing such salubrious nightspots as Hale Methodist Church and Sale Annexe. Eek!

'We did a Cockney Rejects cover,' Squire sheepishly confessed to me in 1995, 'called 'I'm Not A Fool.'' Double eek!

Unsurprisingly, The Patrol were not long for this world. In '81, out of school, Ian and John both moved to Hulme, a notorious tenement estate in central Manchester which was rife with drugs and crime. Brown and Squire began to hang about more with the National Front-hating Gary Mounfield – 'Mani' – and met Cressa (later the Roses dancer and effects man) and Johnny Marr, soon to be a Smith. No longer punks, John was to be seen sporting a Fred Perry casual look, while Ian was hanging with the Chorlton Gladiators scooter gang, and indulging the triplicate passions of Lambrettas, Muhammed Ali and Motown. In an eerie forerunner of the bizarre headgear that Ian Brown would model onstage in 1995, the Gladiators were unmistakable for the rabbit's tail that ran from the front to the back of their helmets – serious boys.

John attended Manchester's Pips club, where different rooms would play Bowie, Roxy, oldies and Northern Soul. Ian's musical horizons were widening also.

'I used to go to Northern Soul all-nighters in Rhyl, Rotherham and Doncaster,' the enigmatic singer told *Q* magazine in 1989. 'Very into it I was. All through the night till late in the morning. It was either that, New Romantics or long raincoats.'

No choice there. Brown's burgeoning musical vocabulary would serve him well in years to come, but few would have suspected a funk or soul influence in the racket of The Patrol! Still, after a short break, thoughts of a group resurfaced. But, alas,

**Squire and Brown . . .**

... friends for as long as they could remember

the Roses' future melodiousness was still nowhere in sight.

'I remember we changed our name to English Rose,' recalled Andy Cousens in *Rock CD*. 'Cos of that Jam track we liked. Bloody diabolical we were! I was on vocals, John was a pretty basic guitar player back then. We were all kicking against it, really, trying to be Manchester's answer to the New York Dolls. People were all going mental about The Smiths, "Oh, this is the best thing since sliced bread", and we f***in' hated it. For us it had to be heavy.'

Oh dear. And just as sadly, English Rose didn't even gig.

So, between 1982 and 1984 John Squire contented himself by fiddling with his amps, guitar and canvas whilst earning a living making models for a childrens TV production of – wait for it – *Wind In the Willows*, whilst Ian Brown's scooter fixation continued in earnest, and was possibly the source of the tough, insular gang mentality that would later typify his group. Oh, and the now distinguished Brown's anything but distinguished criminal record.

'The Scooter Boys were not mods,' the blooming Rose told *Melody Maker* in 1990. 'We were a mixture of punks, skins, anyone who had a scooter. I used to see Clinton from Pop Will Eat Itself on scooter runs; we used to get attacked by bikers in Stourbridge (PWEI's home town) till we followed Clinton down an alternative safe route. The police would pull me up wherever I went. I was once fined £20 for having condensation on my speedometer.'

Blimey. Things just weren't going well at all. Poor Ian had no job, no group and was palpably unprepared for a life of crime. What could he do? Well, the time would come for bigger and better things; enter the hand of fate in the form of a dodgy promoter Ian met by chance over in Germany.

'Yeah, I was hitching around Europe and I met this promoter who said that he could get us some gigs in Sweden,' Brown told *Melody Maker,* in the same interview. 'So obviously we jumped at the chance.'
And who wouldn't ?!

## UP, UP AND AWAY!

EXCITED at the prospect of a free holiday, Brown returned to Blighty and hastily regrouped the band. Out was Simon Wolstencroft (he'd initially left to team up with Marr and Andy Rourke in the pre-Smiths Freak Party, only to leave them, thus cementing a reputation as Manchester's Pete Best). With Ian assuming leadership and vocal duties, in came a hairy goth type called Pete Garner, who'd previously found gainful employment at a stationers called Paperchase. When Alan 'Reni' Wren (10.4.64, Aries) joined through an ad, the fledgling Roses began their ascent into the perfect group. Reni, it turned out, had met Squire and Brown at the age of 11, when he bullied them for 10p at the Belle Vue speedway track.

'I thought they made a horrible racket but I was struck by their commitment,' said the sticksman, explaining his motives in *MM*, 1990. 'The whole group was such an oddball collection of long hairs, scruffs and smoothies that I just had to join.' And they just had to have him. Reni's spiralling, multi-rhythmical drumming (he'd taught himself to play by copying jazz styles in the basement of his father's pub) was to be one of the defining ingredients of the Stone Roses' new musical language. But, before that, came Sweden. Rejecting the name The Angry Young Teddy Bears, the band adopted the similarly rough/smooth moniker The Stone Roses, partly filched from their now favourite pop group, The Rolling Stones. Cousens was still in the band, but his hand was edging towards the exit button.

'Ian was getting mobbed 'cos he'd shaved his hair off and looked really pretty,' said Andy, describing the band's five Scandinavian dates in *Rock CD*. 'It didn't change him but it began to make me think that things were definitely beginning to get a bit tinny and stupid.'

Mobbed?? What Cousens omitted to explain was that at one of the gigs – advertised, illogically but brazenly, in the UK music press – only four people turned up! A far cry from the later mega-gigs at Spike Island and Feile Festival. However, the Swedish gigs did include an early, skeletal version of 'I Wanna Be Adored' and 'This Is The One'. Back in England, The Roses played their first UK gig at an anti-heroin benefit at London's Rock Garden in summer '84. In the audience and later on the stage was none other than The Who's Pete Townshend.

'He came flying over after the set and gushed about how it reminded him of the early Who,' remembered Andy Cousens. 'We were all arrogant little shits and weren't impressed or pretended we weren't anyway. We were all sitting there cursing him, "Pete Townshend, you f\*\*\*in' deaf old bastard, get off!" Pete Townshend's inestimable hooter was not the last famous nose to be put out of joint by the cocky, narcissistic Roses. Nevertheless, no amount of surly brashness was going to stop Reni sneaking up to join the Whoster for encores of 'Substitute' and 'Pictures Of Lily'.

*Something* was starting to come together, but what?

## WAREHOUSE SONGS AND STORIES

SUDDENLY, The Stone Roses hit upon a brainwave which would prove to be an early stroke of genius. They would organise their own gigs! Hence, on a hot summer night in 1984 the fledgling foursome appeared at a party under an old railway arch near Manchester's Piccadilly station. The band took the 'stage' (more likely a load of old boxes) and played songs like 'Heart On The Staves' and 'Gettin' Plenty': driven, heartfelt melodic rock songs that at least showed an inkling of what was to come. The party was such a success that the Roses organised similar warehouse parties in 1985, providing illicit, latenight hang-outs for the many pleasure-seekers piling out of Manchester's Hacienda and looking for somewhere else to chill. Fellow Mancunians New Order had already taken an 'alternative' guitar audience towards the dancefloor, but the Roses were probably the first guitar band to organise what were effectively illegal raves, providing an early glimpse of what would become their symbiotic relationship with underground club culture. Proper times, they were.

'We had a big Rasta who brought his collection in, took over the turntable, said "I'm DJing now," Ian told *Select*. 'He was about six foot five and so everyone said, 'Yeah. Alright!'

'They were packed out' a nostalgic Brown recollected the warehouse days to *Sounds* in 1990. At the first one there was about a thousand people – it was where we got our crowd from.'

With similar astuteness, the Roses were beginning to understand the importance of generating publicity. One day in 1985, the band made the front page of the *Manchester Evening News* after half the concrete buildings in Manchester were suddenly festooned with the legend 'STONE ROSES'. Letters of revulsion filled the local press.

'People just had this preconceived idea that we were hooligans at the time,' remembered Ian Brown in 1990. 'So we were blamed for the graffiti thing. I don't know why everyone got so upset. It was just some mates. We didn't know about it until afterwards. We know who did it but we're not tellin.'

Whatever the true source of the outrageously mischievous street art, it had a positive aspect for the Roses as they were offered a recording opportunity with the tiny independent Thin Line label of Mancunian producer Martin Hannett. Some years earlier, Martin had achieved near-legendary status on the strength of his work with Joy Division, A Certain Ratio and New Order. He was down on his luck by the mid-Eighties but the Roses' introduction to him (by then sometime Roses' manager Howard 'Ginger' Jones) proved to be another formative incident in their development.

'He taught us how to arrange our songs and how to pull our melodies out,' Ian Brown related in an '87 interview. Perhaps the influence (subconsciously???) went further. That unforgettable, echo-laden intro to 'I Wanna Be Adored' on the band's 1989 John Leckie-produced debut album is pure Hannett, whilst Reni's revolving, hypnotic drumbeat on 'I Am The Resurrection' is

almost a carbon copy of the drum pattern on ACR's 1980 'Winter Hill', itself – gulp – a Hannett production. Later, and characteristically, The Stone Roses would deny having learnt anything from Martin. Indeed, from the first moments of their early fame, they would adopt an almost Stalinesque approach to rewriting – or refusing to reveal – their own history.

P'raps we shouldn't blame 'em. 'So Young' b/w 'Tell Me', in August '85, was sadly devoid of the lightness of touch of later releases, being typified by pounding drums, half-developed guitar riffs and histrionic vocals. It gained little attention, although *NME's* Mat Snow did have this to say:

'The great lost Martin Hannett produced this record, and a right silk purse it is too. Pure post-punk 'pocalypse, of course, but even that won't persuade me to play it again.'

Oh dear. Speaking in '89, Ian Brown was similarly dismissive of his group's first attempt at a recording. 'The single was horrible,' the newly-crowned rock God told *MM* in a rare revealing moment. 'We didn't even like it then. Angst-ridden rock.'

Already, the single was selling for £20.

'I'd pay 20p,' spat Ian, with typical Mancunian thrift. Nowadays, it fetches over a hundred, so if Mr. Brown did ever pay 20p he'd have made more than a tidy profit!

Around this time, Ian Brown's already impressive musical vocabulary began to explode, something confirmed by Martin Hannett in various interviews since.

The Roses had been inspired by punk's 'Anyone can do it' ethos, but...

'Punk stopped you listening to stuff like Hendrix and then years later you hear 'Electric Ladyland' and it's an excellent LP,' Ian Brown explained to *Q* magazine in 1989. 'But at the time you don't listen to it because you believe all the bollocks. I wish I'd heard Jimi Hendrix when I was 12.'

Discovering Hendrix was only the beginning. Although far from a scholar earlier in life, Brown's musical education was something he didn't bunk out of.

'For me it's been right through Jackson 5, Motown, Northern Soul,' Ian enthused to

*Sounds* in July '89. 'Then discovering Parliament and Bootsy Collins, then Barry White and Acid House and dance records. Over the same period we had The Beatles, The Rolling Stones, Jimi Hendrix, T. Rex and The Sex Pistols.'

But only later would this admirable openness be heard in his own group's music. Following the spectacular failure of the 'So Young' single, Brown and the boys spent late 1985 working on an album with Martin Hannett. It was never released, but if you ever get to hear the illicit 'First Coming' bootleg, you will hear very primitive stirrings of what was to become the group's sound. Mind you, the leather-trousered, spiky-cropped Brown was – image-wise – still a far cry from the floppy-clobbered Manc rock Adonis of the early Nineties.

The Hannett sessions also proved the final watershed for Andy Cousens.

'I suppose that was the start of the big time for them and the wave goodbye for me,' Cousens told *Rock CD* in 1991. 'We did the 12" with Martin and about four weeks later he came flying over in his usual drugged state and just managed to babble out 'I've booked Strawberry studios for six weeks, let's do some stuff.' We did about 14 tracks, mixed 'em. Ian and I were going in the wrong directions. I had different ideals and we argued a hell of a lot... if you look at them now it fits, they fit together and I didn't fit really. The last time I saw them was at Martin Hannett's funeral.' Complete with Pete Garner's booming goff basslines and Ian's angsty wailings, the Roses of the Hannett sessions sounded like another mid-Eighties Manchester group, The Chameleons. Indeed, an apocryphal story has it that around this time a Geffen Records A & R executive had heard of a hard-hitting, melodic rock band causing some ripples around Manchester and was promptly despatched to investigate The Stone Roses. Arriving at a typically sweatladen gig, he was sufficiently impressed to offer the band a two album deal: possibly the reason why the resolutely indie Chameleons ended up on Geffen. Yup, he'd signed the wrong band!

**The Stone Roses' first manager Howard Jones and (overleaf) the International Club, Manchester**

## MOVING ON UP

IF 1985 was again largely characterised by disappointments and disasters, 1986 proved to be a watershed. This was the year that The Stone Roses hooked up with Gareth Evans, a wide boy and eccentric of considerable disrepute, but also an accountant and owner of Manchester's two notorious International clubs. In an eerie parallel with Ian Brown and John Squire's Sex Pistols-crazy youth, Evans would become to the Roses what Malcolm McLaren was to the Sex Pistols: a Svengali figure who would catapult the band to international fame before ending up being jettisoned by the band in a rash of litigation and ill-feeling. More of *that* later. At the time of their initial meeting, he was trading in novelty underpants and apparently dropped his trousers as part of his sales patter to try and get the Roses to buy a few pairs. Perhaps they should have been a little more wary of him!

Nevertheless, Gareth Evans had a critical input as he instigated crucial changes to the band. At the same time, out went Andy Cousens and in came Gary Mounfield – 'Mani', John and Ian's National Front-baiting mate of their teenage years. Furthermore, Gareth's offer of free rehearsal time at his club benefited the band considerably, as did the experience of seeing the pure pop Primal Scream at their early, jangling zenith. This was to be a turning point for the Roses – inspired by Bobby Gillespie's group's twanging, Byrdsy melodies and heart-racing choruses, they began to craft a far bouncier, tuneful sound than they'd ever hinted at, accompanied by newly-ironed paisley shirts. As the music softened in important places, the band's attitude was hardening.

'Being ignored by the biz for years didn't make us stronger,' John Squire reflected to me in 1995. 'But it highlighted the strengths that we already had, if you're willing to carry on when nobody seems interested. We did create a certain amount of self-belief.'

Within months, it was clear to everyone who had the good fortune to hear them that they'd be unstoppable. Time to fasten those safety belts, the Roses were taking off.

# This is the One

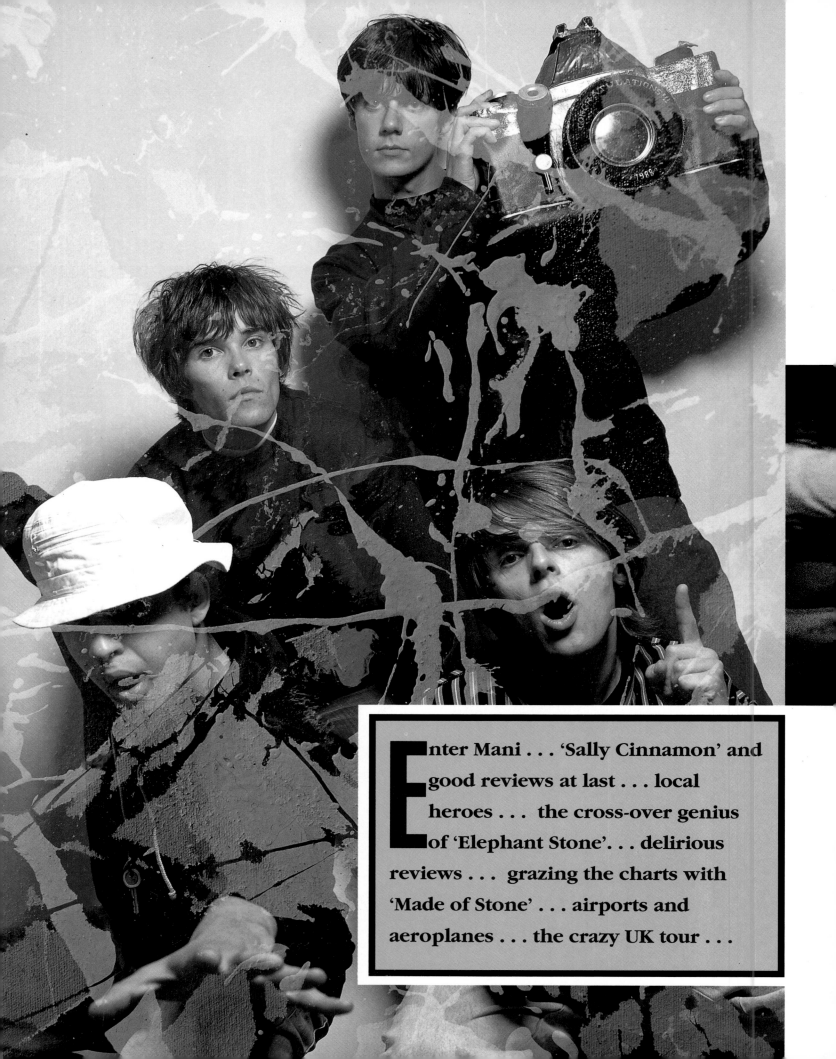

Enter Mani . . . 'Sally Cinnamon' and good reviews at last . . . local heroes . . . the cross-over genius of 'Elephant Stone'. . . delirious reviews . . . grazing the charts with 'Made of Stone' . . . airports and aeroplanes . . . the crazy UK tour . . .

## EVANS ABOVE

GARETH Evans set about pestering local journos and attempting to gain interest from record companies. Also, just as importantly, the group now played almost exclusively in Manchester, creating enormous interest locally and meaning that if A & R types from London wanted a piece of the action they'd have to burn rubber on the motorway. As the band's following expanded, so did the music, taking on increasing psychedelic qualities, dazzling liquid guitar runs and Ian's newly aquired airy vocals (a benefit of singing lessons). Then, in July '87, came the first great Stone Roses record, 'Sally Cinnamon',

ovation. The Roses are to The Stones what The Smiths are to The Beatles, a collision of rock, pop and psychedelia.' *MM's* Penny Kiley raved about their Sefton Park, Liverpool show (where they were – whisper it – upstaged by The La's), saying 'Next big things. Brattish pop in psychedelic clothes.'

But while Manchester's *Evening News* went one further, stating 'Love or loathe the Roses, they should be huge on the stadium circuit,' the group were still painfully broke, Reni earning a few quid by donning stockings, suspenders and a skirt and working as a kissogram!

Still, the world was starting to listen.

poised and pristine, it surfed along on a wave of glorious melody and a nimble, pulsating dance groove, subsiding only for Ian's dizzying vocal punchline ('*Seems like there's a hole in my dreams*'). On this beautiful record, the first to be encased in John Squire's paint-splattered artwork, the Roses had arrived – fully formed and original – but unlike the fans in Manchester, the London music press were slow to recognise what lay before them.

Edwyn Pouncey of *NME* mystifyingly suggested the reader should stick with The Velvet Underground's 'Sister Ray', while *Record Mirror* wrote, more damningly, 'If

a delicious stew of cloudgrazing melody and lovestruck vocal intentions.

Sadly, the single didn't receive any national reviews, however after a gig at this time, *Sounds'* Stephen Kingston summed up Ian and the Roses' unique appeal thus:

'He's whirling around the stage like a demented muppet crooning to no one in particular, he does fancy himself as a bit of a star and you want to hate the guy. The songs are so mellifluous though, that somehow you just get sucked in.'

Also in *Sounds,* Mancunian journo John Robb described 'A Man' United-style terrace

### ELEPHANT'S RAVEYARD

EARLY in '88 the group entered Suite 16 studios in Rochdale to record 'Elephant Stone' with New Order's Peter Hook producing. Sadly, Rough Trade, who had been planning to release the record, mysteriously pulled out, leaving the band with a finished single and no record company. Eventually Andrew Lauder (former Buzzcocks A & R man at United artists) stepped in and made the Roses the first signing to his new Silvertone label.

'Elephant Stone', released in October '88, was a world class pop record. Euphoric,

they would only look beyond Lancashire, beyond indie-land itself, they'll realise there's more to life than lollipops, psychedelia and flakey grey skin.'

Ouch. Only the local press were supportive, *M62's* Andrew McQueen's hitting the nail somewhere about the head when he said 'Every Roses' song has a melody that tugs at your heartstrings and 'Elephant Stone' is no exception. Fresh as a daisy but vitally urgent, the guitar explores every nook and cranny of the song, exploiting every melodic opportunity to the hilt. What's more, unlike many leaden-booted guitar bands, The

Stone Roses have a groove and percussive sway that grips your hips and won't let go. There's just a buzz and attitude around them that's so exciting. Single Of The Year.'

Oh yes. On the 12" B-side, 'Full Fathom Five' explored the delights of reverse mixing and studio wizardry, hinting at the tricks that, shortly afterwards, would help to create their revolutionary debut album. Sadly, though,

Towards the end of '88, The Stone Roses could be seen in a tiny hall at Central London Polytechnic playing with Chameleons offshoot The Sun And The Moon to a handful of disinterested students.

'If I thought we were going to remain selling 2,000 records I'd give in now,' Ian Brown admitted to Manchester journalist Sarah Champion, 'but I seriously think we're

important people. The first was a devoted superfan, the first of thousands, with 'The Stone Roses' scrawled down one side of her denim jacket and 'Jimi Hendrix Experience' on the other. The second was Bob Stanley of Nineties nouveau ice cool existentialist disco outfit Saint Etienne, back then the mere Bob Stafford, a young and refreshingly excitable *Melody Maker* journalist.

**Ian and John with Jackson Pollock-inspired guitars**

the single sold poorly, entering the indie chart at a mere Number 27 and selling almost all copies in and around Manchester. At this time, local group Inspiral Carpets paid tribute to the Roses on their 'Plane Crash' debut EP, with 'Garage Full Of Flowers' (an old Brown lyric). But would the Roses suffer the same fate as The Chameleons and (for many years) James, who became huge in Manchester but whose following failed to translate to a nationwide stage?

going to be huge. You can't keep a good band down.'

Or a great song, and the Roses had just written one: 'Made Of Stone'.

### TIMES FLIGHT

IN early 1989, The Stone Roses hauled themselves around the country, playing to 12 people in Cardiff and a mere 10 in Hull. In the audience at one gig, at Middlesex Polytechnic in North London were two very

Bob was blown away. He had seen the future of rock 'n' roll and, no, it was definitely not called Bruce.

'They sound like someone sneaked a tab into your Tizer,' he babbled the following week. 'They sound like the best thing I ever heard, maybe. I'm agog. The Stone Roses... Jesus *Christ*.'

Stafford wasn't alone in his fervour. *NME's* Andrew Collins saw the band's seminal March 1989 Hacienda gig and

**Left, right, far right, ICA London, April 1989**

declared: 'I'm already drafting a letter to my grandchildren telling them that I saw The Stone Roses at the Hacienda... The Stones (and *there's* a clue), comprising four unassuming boy wonders and a Happy Mondays roadie acting as 'surf' dancing accessory, and playing thoroughly regardless brat-arsed guitar Pop, have taken at least four years off my age. 'I Wanna Be Adored' is awesome, spooky and pleading. These brightest of sparks actually do merit your adoration.'

Out of nowhere (and, unknown to their converts, after five years hard slog) The Stone Roses had emerged with a Sound, a Look and their own Myth for their taking. The Hacienda show (parts of which were broadcast on BBC2's *Snub TV*) was one turning point, 'Made Of Stone' was another. Their second aweinspiringly dizzying 45, it hit the shops in March and the listener right

in the cerebral cortex. Even the national reviewers at last took note. Although *MM's* Ian Gittins likened the single to plod-rock wailers Spear Of Destiny, John Robb – who else? – recognised 'a masterpiece', whilst *Record Mirror* declared, 'Everyone who seems to care says that Manchester's Stone Roses are the next *very* big thing. On this evidence, they are certainly contenders. Despite bearing an uncanny resemblance to Primal Scream's 'Velocity Girl', 'Made Of Stone' is honest pop music at its most celebratory, complete with a detachable chorus and optional Seventies guitar effects.'

Also important was national air-play, and Radio One's Richard Skinner was one of a few DJs to champion the band. I can still remember hearing 'Made Of Stone' for the first time, trickling across the late night airwaves, a melody strong enough to launch ships from and a vocal line pure enough to

melt the hardest heart.

'*Sometimes I fantasise/when the streets are cold and lonely and the cars they burn below me/Are you all alone?/Is anybody home?'*

Pretty soon now, everyone would find their fantasies alive in the music of The Stone Roses. To accompany the release of the single, the band gave an interview to *Melody Maker's* superfan Bob Stafford, where Ian Brown revealed all about the group's love affair with sound and the unusual, hallucinatory ambient sequence of the B-side, 'Guernica'.

'We go to Manchester airport in the summer,' Ian whispered conspiratorially, 'and watch the planes land and take off. Your eardrums feel like they're shredding with the volume of the engines. And the fire coming out the back. It's an awesome sight, 30 feet from a plane. We want to get that sound

onto record – bits of 'Guernica' sound like planes, but it's just 'Made Of Stone' backwards with forward vocals. I'd love to have done it as an A-side.'

In the same interview, the Roses spoke about their love for Hendrix, Isaac Hayes, Kojak and Steve McQueen. And what of other, current groups?

'The only other group that matters are Happy Mondays,' insisted Ian,. 'We went to see them at the Astoria and this mad f***er from Glasgow comes up to us and says "Are you The Stone Roses? Got any E?" And a bit later three lads from Leeds come over, same thing. Thanks to The Stone Roses, and their increasing fame, it seemed as though Manchester was fast becoming the Haight Ashbury of the Eighties!

Manchester, Ecstasy and The Stone Roses: in the media eyeview, the three would soon be inseparable.

## STONE LOVE

'MADE Of Stone' breached the national Top One-hundred and entered the indie charts at Number Four.

Then, during May, the Stone Roses embarked on a short tour of the UK – generating a level of excitement that just had to be seen to be believed.

'You've got to see this amazing group from Manchester,' raved my friend Choque (now of dub experimentalists Black Star Liner), whose group The Hollow Men were supporting the Roses. 'I've never seen anything like it.'

Two nights later, May 8 1989, I saw the Roses at Leeds Warehouse and was blown away. The atmosphere was electric and the music poured out of the speakers like a waterfall of melody. People were dancing on the tables. And the band – in baggy, bright T-shirts and wider-than-wide jeans – seemed

to have such an unnatural, startling presence. When a chant of 'We are Leeds' went up as an attempt to goad a gaggle of Manchester fans, Ian Brown simply smiled, shrugged and stated

'This is Leeds'.

The band effortlessly launched into 'I Wanna Be Adored' and the situation was instantly defused.

The next day, I penned a rabid, awestruck review for my then fanzine, *Avanti!:*

'The best band in the world...' I gurgled. 'And no encore. Even the Stone Roses couldn't follow THAT.'

After their ICA show, also in May, *Melody Maker*'s Everett True was similarly agog.

'The Stone Roses have arrived,' he drools. 'The whole f***ing hype is completely justified.

The hype? Truth was, it had really only just begun.

# Roses in Bloom

## ...AND THE GODS MADE LOVE

THE Stone Roses eponymous LP hit the shops in May of '89 and, simply, trashed the opposition. Aside from a mildly lukewarm reception in *NME*, the reviews bordered on the revelatory.

'In guitar pop terms, this is a masterpiece,' declared *Sounds'* John Robb. 'Who'd have guessed that a gang of scruffy kids thudding away in a freezing rehearsal room could have come up with something this magnificent, beautiful and confident?'

Over at *RM,* Andy Strickland wrote of 'The only young band around at the moment with the potential and the balls to go all the way.' *MM's* Bob Stafford (now using the pen-name Bob Stanley), wrote:

'The spine of the LP is John Squire's guitar playing. Beautifully flowing, certainly psychedelic, there are elements of Hendrix ('Shoot You Down') and Marr ('Bye Bye Badman'), but the rest is the lad's own work. 'Waterfall' is a showcase switching from acoustic to wah-wah to funk without once sounding clumsy. The sweet ache of poignancy... This is a trip.'

Even the staid *Observer* raved of 'jangling in every sense', while America's influential *Rolling Stone* said 'The Stone Roses are blooming in Technicolour.'

'The Stone Roses' album was simply blistering, from the eerie, opening declaration of 'I Wanna Be Adored' to the

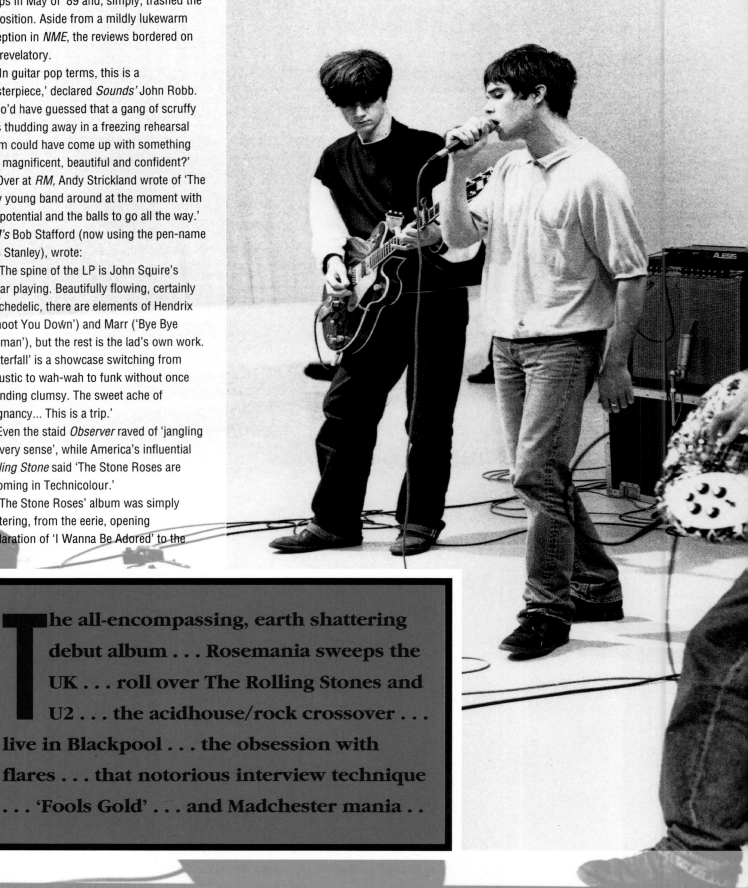

The all-encompassing, earth shattering debut album . . . Rosemania sweeps the UK . . . roll over The Rolling Stones and U2 . . . the acidhouse/rock crossover . . . live in Blackpool . . . the obsession with flares . . . that notorious interview technique . . . 'Fools Gold' . . . and Madchester mania . .

**Backstage at the Blackpool Winter Gardens, 1989**

epic, closing 'I Am The Resurrection', which managed to combine sheer vitriol, biblical imagery ('*I am the resurrection and I am the light*' – inspired by a message on a church noticeboard) and astonishing, tripped-òut guitar frazzles. The album came wrapped inside another delicious John Squire action painting sleeve. Inside and out it was the perfect package and it went on to sell 450,000 copies. Four years later, it was to be voted the singularly greatest album of the Eighties by *Q* magazine. An immortal debut.

Suddenly, Roses fever gave birth to something greater; Roses*mania*. A gig at Leeds Polytechnic on June 30 saw crazed scenes, with fans being locked outside, unparalleled in the venue's history.

*MM's* Simon Reynolds described 'A fountainhead of rapture'.

Before the gig, Ian Brown told me: 'We want to be massive. How massive? Well,

New Order (then on top of the charts and their own world with the 'Technique' album) aren't massive. Michael Jackson, that's *massive*. That's what we're aiming for.'

Some would be put off by the band's outward arrogance and surly behaviour, but the Roses' music more than backed up such outlandish statements. And they knew it. At the height of their early infamy, the Roses turned down the chance to support New Order, The Pixies, a desperate Bros (!) and (gasp) The Rolling Stones.

'The Rolling Stones? They should be bloody supporting us,' Ian insisted to *Q*.

'Mick Jagger? I'd want to punch him out,' he insisted to *NME*. 'There was a time, for three or four years, when The Stones were red hot. They looked good, sounded good and meant what they were playing. Nothing could stop them. Now they're nothing but a money-making machine. Sad really.'

'We never support,' Brown added to Irish music paper *Hot Press.* 'You're joking, why support? That's a no-ambition, to want to warm up for anybody else. It's a waste of time. We supported some people when we started, That Petrol Emotion at the Riverside in '86; a group called Mercenary Skank. But it's prostituting yourself. Once we'd done it, we realised we hated it. We don't do anything that appals us. We do what we think is right.'

Self-belief and principles were beginning to go hand in hand with the Roses. Here was a band who knew exactly what they wanted.

'It's nothing against any of the groups,' the golden Brown explained to *Select.* 'It's just that we don't want to warm up for anyone else. We don't want to be part of someone else's night out. We want it to be a night out, we want to create a night out.'

And they did. Oh yes.

## OPEN UP

IT'S an old, abused cliche, but the Roses did open up the minds of their audience. Their gigs were experiences, beginning long before the band even came on with a booming, hallucinatory House and Acid soundtrack, unheard of at the time. Through them, a generation of indie kids discovered how to dance. The Roses gigs became wild, joyous celebrations of youth, limitless energy and the sound of a million summers.

'I'm not really into white guitar bands,' John Squire told *MM* at the time. 'They're boring. We just listen to all the best stuff – Sex Pistols, Love, Parliament, and right now the 'Shaft' double LP and Adrian Sherwood.'

The Roses were a rock band who were actively rejecting rock 'n' roll tradition.

'I don't see us in a rock 'n' roll tradition at all,' Ian Brown related to *NME*. 'You go to a reggae gig or a punk gig, or an artists' party or maybe just up to Alderly Edge to look out over Manchester, and you'll find people getting into spliffs and brandy. All kinds. That doesn't make them rock 'n' roll. In fact I don't like rock 'n' roll; the attitude and the leather jacket, it's old hat. It's redneck.

'Think about it, all the biggest rock groups in the world are rednecks, white Anglo-Saxons; Bon Jovi, Guns 'N' Roses, U2. The frightening thing is that people all over the world relate to that redneck rubbish. Guns 'N' Roses especially.

'I mean, I read how Guns 'N' Roses were stopped from playing an AIDS benefit because one of the songs on their LP goes on about 'Stupid faggots'. And that album was Number One in America. How far back have we gone when a pop group can put rubbish like that in people's heads?'

The Stone Roses were a Manchester band who were sprinkling a new joy over the city's recent musical past, the climate of bedsit miserablism (intentionally or unintentionally) bred by Joy Division and The Smiths.

'When we're good, I'm totally at ease – with the situation, with myself,' Ian enthused to *Q.* 'You buzz off the music and float off in your own bubble. When we're not good I get bored and I can't get into it. I refuse to fake it, so I come across as a bored, snooty twat. Too bad. Why fake it?'

The music set the band on fire and their increasingly inflammatory rhetoric and strongly held views set the individuals apart in a pop scene that, post-Smiths, had grown stale amid the empty egotism and the false back-slapping of the post-Live Aid era.

'U2?' pondered Ian. 'Drivel. Just crap. They don't sound like they mean it. They sound like they wanna be a famous pop group but forgot about the rest of it.'

Springsteen: 'Nothing for me, all that power and glory chestbeating stuff.' (John)

'Always sounds to me like he's 'avin' a shit.' (Ian)

Lou Reed: 'A miserable bastard.' (Ian)

Just as the shock of the new was sinking in, the summer was to provide the big push from 'underground Manchester band' to *Top Of The Pops* with the immaculate 'She Bangs The Drums', taken from the LP as a single in July, a wild Japanese tour and the announcement of a massive one-off celebratory gig at Blackpool's Empress Ballroom in August.

'She Bangs The Drums' was a truly heart-stopping pop record, racing through the speed of life and in awe of its own magnificence: '*I can feel the earth begin to move/I hear my needle hit the groove/And spiral through another day/I hear my song begin to say/Kiss me where the sun don't shine/The past was yours but the future's mine.*' And then, delivered almost as an afterthought/kiss off: '*You're all out of time.*'

There was no backlash. 'Let's call them the Stones – no one will be confused,' raved *Sounds.* Although *MM* maverick Everett True was quick to point out his preference for the B-side, the lilting 'Standing Here.' 'Epic sweep... sublime glow and polish,' he raved. Surprisingly, the single peaked at 36, dissatisfying the group.

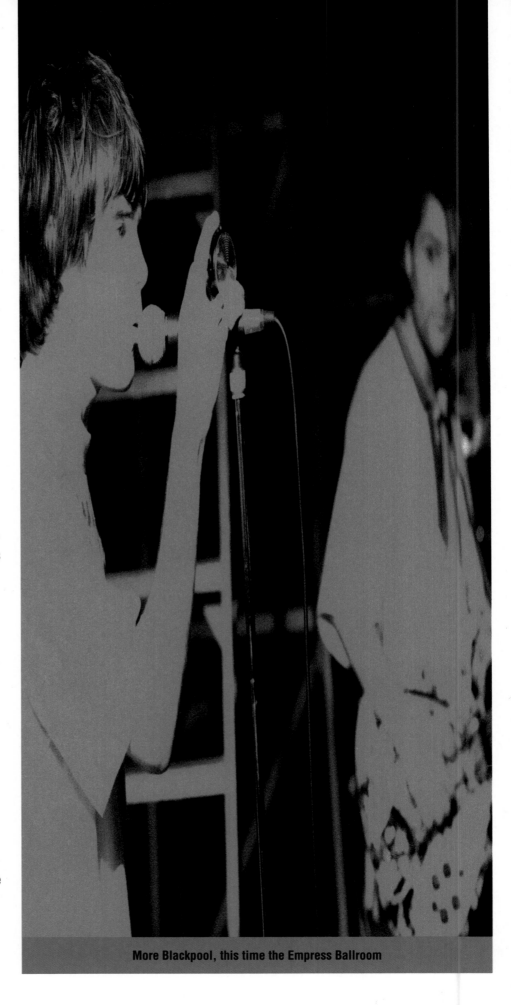

**More Blackpool, this time the Empress Ballroom**

'I'll be severely disappointed if we haven't had a Number One by the end of 1989,' Ian told *Melody Maker*. 'Cos the time is right. Anything's possible.'

Yeah, it seemed like anything *was* possible. A number 36 was but a temporary glitch.

The 4,000-capacity Blackpool Empress Ballroom gig was a Stone classic, capturing the dazzling, boundary-smashing Roses at their white hot, immaculate zenith whilst perhaps casting a sly throwback to Ian and John's scooter-riding seaside days. Prior to the gig, Ian Brown told *NME*:

'I'm dying to get on. There's a great atmosphere. 4,000 people have come here for the day; hung out on the fair and the beach; gonna go and see the Stone Roses; and then go and have a party.'

He also provided a rare glimpse of his acutely sensitive nature, the boy idealist of lovelorn, gentle songs like 'Standing Here' and 'Going Down'.

'We went to see a dolphin in Brighton,' he whispered. 'It was really sad because it was in a tiny little pool. None of us said anything for about half-an-hour. We just stared at it. It kept going past and turning it's head and smiling. It didn't jump up at anybody else, though, did it? There were loads of people around the pool and it kept circling only jumping up when it saw us.'

The journalist then reports 'Ian falls into a complete depression.'

Such mood swings are still an integral part of Ian's complex character. Within seconds, prior to going onstage, he said, 'It's where you're at that counts. And we're going all the way to the top.'

Brown's renewed enthusiasm was not misplaced. Afterwards, *Melody Maker's* Bob Stanley reviewed the Big Day Out in Blackpool thus:

'For most people here this has been *the* event on the summer calendar and it's been organised as such, set in the tinsel heart of the tackiest summer resort in the country. The atmosphere is raw E. The Salem witch trials were nothing on this. The Stone Roses appear and their appeal is instant and obvious; simultaneously they look like anyone and they look untouchable, four blokes in the Stretford End and four teenage Jesus Christs. Pop perfection.'

Not to be outdone, *NME* described 'the future, the resurrection. A personification of the changing tide of feeling that's sweeping the country and filling every last crevice of this gilt-mirrored seaside palace. Shitty sound and whatever other disadvantages aside, you know even before The Stone Roses put one foot on that stage that you wouldn't take a million-zillion pounds to be anywhere else.'

Phew!

## FLARE UP

FOR the first time, the Empress Ballroom gig marked the coming together of The Stone Roses and their audience in spirit and (ahem) sartorial elegance. Clad in flared trousers, cords and outsize Italian and Spanish casual tops as modelled by Ian, Mani and John and floppy fisherman's hats as worn by Reni, the audience looked like an invasion. They took over the sleepy seaside town, one nation under a big and decidedly humungous *baggy* groove.

'Someone got me to write "Ian Brown 12/8/89" down their leg,' exclaimed a horrified Ian, loath to 'ruin' someone's bonzer new pair of strides.

'I can't understand it,' rued John. 'They're wearing good clobber, some of them and they want us to destroy it.'

From here on in, the words 'Stone Roses' and 'flares' would be almost inseparable.

However...

'I'm the only one who wears flares,' Brown told *NME*. 'The rest wear parallels. We're *obsessed* with clothes. Always have been. It's all very important: like, for instance – and make sure you get this right – with flares coming back people have got to realise that you can't wear anything wider than Twenty-one inch bottoms. Anything more looks ridiculous.'

Rumour has it the original source of Ian's flared green cords was shaven-headed Roses 'dancer' and John Squire's effects pedal operative, the enigmatic Cressa.

**Reni behind the drumkit**

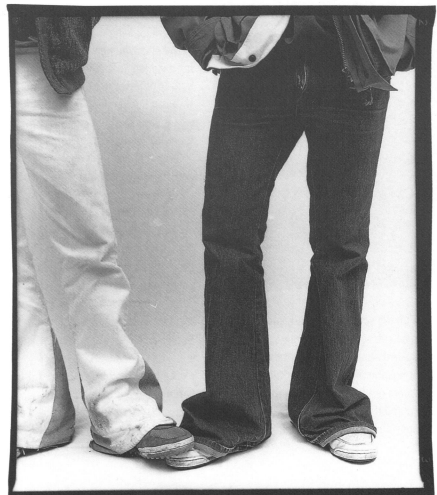

'I used to knock around with Cressa a lot back in '84,' the floppy-fringed John told *Sounds,* 'and we all used to be well into flares then'

'John had twenty-four inch cotton drill,' Ian confirmed. 'You get a buzz out of it. Because people look at you and laugh because they're not wearing the same pants. It's weird how something so simple can make you feel really special.'

Just as soon as their entire audience were clad in flares or, more dubiously 'parallels', the Roses would stop wearing them.

## STONEWALLING ROSES

BY now the music press were mad for the Roses. Barely a week went by without some article or other detailing their activities and views. Did I say 'detailing'?! Most Roses interviews were remarkable for covering large areas of space without really saying anything. Their past was almost a no-go area, their present largely dealt with in enigmatic halfquotes, statements of intent and, very occasionally, a rare anecdote.

*Sounds* described the Roses' interview technique thus:

'At the push of a record button the friendly Roses become laconic, bolshy boys. Specialities include needless semantics, and the old turning-the-question-back-on-the-interviewer gambit. The Stone Roses' unwillingness, or inability, to talk at great length is a symptom of their strength. They come with no agenda, no press manifesto and are free from the mannered rock referencing that's plagued rock recently.'

Another, uncredited article in the band's hardly illuminating press file is less even-handed. 'They are far from indifferent to the prospect of getting publicity,' the journalist reports. 'On three separate occasions during the three-hour interview their conversation becomes so vague and incoherent that I press the pause button and tell them there is no point continuing. Each time they plead with me to stay.'

Was there any reasoning behind such awkward, uncommunicative behaviour?

'After the first few interviews we were

getting pressurised to open up and be more chatty,' John revealed to *Sounds.* 'Sell yourself, treat it as a PR exercise. And we've resisted it.'

'So we weren't talking,' Ian carried on, 'and people around us, press officers, said 'You can't do that, you won't be getting anymore interviews. People won't want to talk to you cos you're not saying anything. And about three weeks later it's "Ooh, it's working. What a great angle."

'It's not an angle. It's *us.*

'We don't think about the image we put across. Honest,' Ian insisted to *Q.* 'I just try and be myself for as many hours of the day as possible. I'm conscious of not wanting to slip into ego-trip territory which, from an outside point of view watching groups come up, it's easy to do. If that happened I'd just sack it because you stop achieving anything. How will I recognise that point? Because I know that I've got friends who'd give me a slap around the face. Kick me arse. *Behave*, you know. It's the easiest thing in the world to just sink into it. "We just came to rock 'n' roll" and all that bollocks.'

The Roses claim never to have had heroes (with the exception, of Ian, who cites one or two boxers). *Melody Maker's* Simon Reynolds described 'a natural manner somewhere between the deadpan wit of Beatles and the mordant intransigence of The Sex Pistols. Perhaps the Roses had studied their rock history? Maybe, even, they'd taken tips from Gareth Evans, their calculated, shrewd manager.

'I gave them their mystique,' Evans once claimed. 'Look at other bands. When they come off stage, they mix with their fans. You shouldn't do that.'

Speaking to *Sounds,* John offered a more straightforward truth.

'If you're talking to a dickhead then you're not going to give much of yourself away,' he stated, 'and it's bound to be a chore.'

There could be little doubt that The Roses were a band who knew what they were about, and mostly they sought trust. After all, couldn't we trust them, to up the ante? And they would. Oh yes.

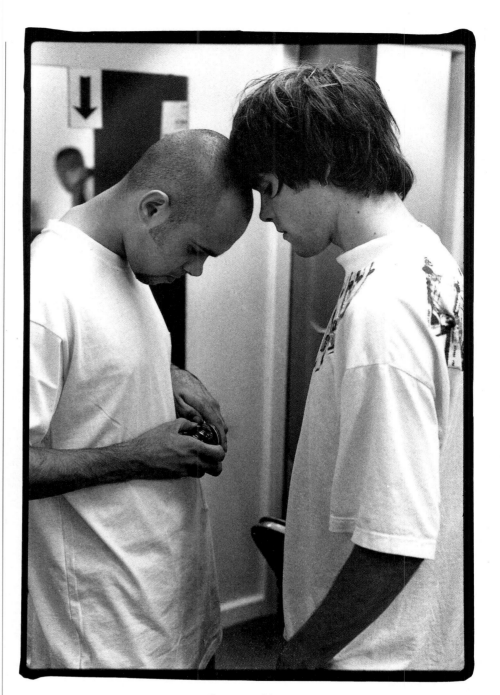

**Cressa and Ian**

## GOING FOR GOLD

IN a career littered with highpoints, November '89 was a milestone. The Roses new single, 'Fools Gold', was their boldest move to date, a hypnotic slab of smouldering pop funk with a liquid, shuffling drum 'n' bass chassis highlighted by the appearance of an irresistibly nimble, melodic bassline. 'Fools Gold' confirmed what many had suspected: that here was a four-square guitar rock band with an intrinsic understanding of dance culture. The Roses weren't merely mimicking that culture – otherwise they'd have delivered a 120 BPM, keyboard smothered hardfloor stomper – but they were assimilating it, breathing it, absorbing dancefloor grooves.

'We wouldn't say "Let's write a funk song",' Ian affirmed in *Melody Maker.* 'We might end up like The Stones, man. Trying to sound black. My favourite records at the moment are reggae and I wouldn't think about making a reggae record. When bands think they can do anything it's shit.'

Despite their bold announcements, the Roses were obviously aware of their own limitations but massively exploited their strengths. In terms of progression and sheer, unrivalled brilliance, 'Fools Gold' left the Roses' previous attempt at dancefloor compatibility – 'Elephant Stone' – far behind, with the rest of the competition. It was, truly, a milestone record.

'The Stone Roses are perfect: aware of the need for pop to recognise an R & B past and a technological present, they write songs of mystery, use slithering breakbeats and fearlessly deliver tight records of depth and insight,' raved *NME*. 'This record gives the term psychedelic soul a new meaning: this is what the 13th Floor Elevators would have sounded like if they were less into tuning in, turning on and dropping out, and more into James Brown. Wah-wah guitars, thin, laconic voices, deadly Clyde Stubblefield drums and a drifting, humane mix. Thirteen minutes of pure pleasure.'

'Fools Gold' came wrapped in another delicious John Squire sleeve with painting insert, 'Double Dorsal Doppleganger One', a gold... dolphin. The flip delivered the gorgeous, jogging pop groove of 'What The World Is Waiting For', a track which exemplified the Roses' knack of creating seemingly *effortless* brilliance.

The reviews for 'Fools Gold' were ecstatic, right across the board. Meanwhile, the pop media were full of stories of the Pop/Acid House crossover, something that left Ian Brown non-plussed.

'We were always into dance music,' he explained. 'Rock and dance were always side by side as far as I am concerned. People have this way of categorising. It's ridiculous really. The reason we didn't do a dance thing earlier was that we probably couldn't have handled it. If we'd have had more experience, the first LP would sound more like 'Fools Gold' than it does, cos we see all those songs as being dance tracks. When we play them live everyone is dancing to them. So 'Fools Gold' didn't seem like a sudden change for us. it was just the natural thing to do at the time.'

The other Madchester big leaguers of 1987, Happy Mondays

## MANCHESTER UNITED?

'FOOLS Gold'/'What The World Is Waiting For' entered the charts at Number Fourteen, peaking at Number Eight. That week, The Stone Roses and fellow Mancunian guitar pop shufflers Happy Mondays appeared together on *Top Of The Pops*. It was a defining moment that would signify the times and stay in people's memories for many years to come.

While the Roses slid through 'Fools Gold', the Mondays (as they were now being called) performed 'Hallelujah' from their 'Madchester Rave On' EP, titled in tribute to the crazed, colourful pop phenomenon emerging out of the city. Indeed, the music media were beginning to talk in terms of a 'Holy Triumvirate' of the Roses, the Mondays, and similarly emerging Mancunian pop outfit Inspiral Carpets. Although, with hindsight, the loveable Inspirals could hardly be put in the same bracket, being an efficient, if not particularly inspired pop outfit; a hybrid of Sixties psychedelics The Seeds, erstwhile punks The Stranglers and early Eighties keyboard-drenched pop group The Teardrop Explodes.

Roses-influenced groups were emerging

Manchester. This is now.'

If *this* was to be Manchester, the Roses, sensibly, wanted nothing to do with it.

'We might come from Manchester but we don't see ourselves as a continuation of any Manchester scene,' Ian Brown told *NME*. 'The world doesn't begin and end at The Hacienda and we're interested in reaching the rest of the world.'

Interestingly, when Granada TV began filming for a proposed 'Madchester' documentary, The Stone Roses were the sole absentees.

'Manchester really matters but we don't need to promote it,' a slightly more considerate Ian told *Select*. 'We want Manchester to have the 1996 Olympics cos we think it's right. You know, we support Manchester if you like. But we also support other places like Glasgow, Belfast, London, Liverpool, anywhere where people try and do their own thing.'

In another parallel to The Sex Pistols success/notoriety of a decade or more earlier, it became apparant that not enough of the flare-wearing followers or soundbite-hunting media pack seemed to understand that if The Stone Roses were about anything, they were about individuality, respect, and personal liberation.

'I believe in anarchy,' John Squire explained to *Interview* magazine. 'By anarchy I don't mean going around smashing things up or clubbing grannies. Just personal freedom for everybody.'

'Happy Mondays?' John pondered in *Sounds*. I'm sure there are a lot of similarities in attitude, but we're not joined at the hip 'We've never gone out of our way to align ourselves to the so-called Manchester scene, 'Ian reiterated. 'We've never understood the supposed connection between us and all these other bands. It's a media thing. Everyone's talking about rock and dance coming together all of a sudden. Well that's bollocks! Everyone I know has always listened to both kinds of music. It's not a sudden thing that's happened. It's just that the media has now decided to tie it up into a neat little package and made it

around the nation, such as The Bridewell Taxis and The Inept (Leeds), Northside, Asia Fields, Rig and The Madjacks (Manchester) and, most notably, The Charlatans, who were based in and around the Midlands but who didn't exactly challenge the preconception of them as a Manchester act. Indeed, The Charlatans were the most Roses soundalike of all and actively used the Roses (who they supported on several occasions) as a springboard for their own success. Before long, acts such as the Inspirals, Mancunian Techno outfit 808 State and long-serving popsters James would all be able to fill huge

venues, largely as a result of the interest in the 'Manchester phenomenon'. Later, the Charlatans, too, would develop their sound and enjoy considerable success, but for now there was the distinct feeling of a bandwagon being leapt upon. Much of the talk of a 'Manchester scene' seemed like shameless opportunism: from the pop media (enjoying a surge in interest), to the bands (many of whom were woefully lacking in their own inspiration), to the entrepreneurs, such as the Joe Bloggs clothing retailer who brandished a crisp pair of flared jeans on television with the words 'This is

acceptable. People are people and your attitude is your attitude. It ain't where you come from, it's where you're at, right!'

This last comment would become a famous soundbite, used to illustrate pictures of the Roses everywhere from the teenage press to the national dailies.

But once again, The Stone Roses were ahead of the game.

## EVERYTHING STARTS WITH AN 'E'

IN the hazy, heady days of the Roses' explosion, personal freedom, for a lot of people, meant one thing: an Ecstasy tablet. The times indeed were-a-changin'. The Berlin wall was about to tumble and on a more domestic note, the twin evils of SAW pop and bloated stadium rock which had ruled for so long were in the process of being banished. Maybe it was the new decade that lay around the corner, maybe it was the heady delirium, the *power* within the Roses music and the increasing overlaps between the introspection of rock and the hedonism of dance. Or maybe it was just the drugs.

But for a lot of people, there was a feeling of a new openness, that Things Would Never Be The Same Again.

'Ecstasy and House music seemed to raise a lot of people to another level,' Ian Brown told *Interview* magazine shortly after the band broke big. 'People who'd maybe be out fighting and drinking beer. It calmed 'em down, chilled 'em out. It brought people up, made 'em more aware, opened their eyes.'

'But we were there without the drug,' insisted Mani.

'I lived music before those days,' the bassist told me in *I-D* in '95. 'We were never Timothy Leary types. As for being 'The acid house group The Stone Roses', then, no.'

Maybe not. But at the time...

'Ecstasy! Ecstasy! We're gonna dance like... *fish*,' *Q* magazine reported Mani as yelling, in a Stockholm nightclub. And an illuminating quote leapt out from those days. Manager Gareth Evans remarked, 'These boys get through a lot of drugs'.

'Gareth Evans wouldn't know what we got up to,' spat Mani to me, in '95. 'We've had

**Windswept on Blackpool promenade, August '89**

**Ian and John fooling around before the Blackpool Winter Gardens gig**

our moments, I can't deny it. Everyone likes a little go at... trips or something. It's just a young thing innit?'

Just a young thing? For many in '89, the music of the Roses went hand in hand with the Ecstasy and House experience. It was a blurring of the boundaries, a blurring of the edges between fantasy and a new reality. E, House, the Roses and an unusually hot summer just added to the feeling that *something* was happening. But what?

'What happened reaffirmed to us what we always thought could happen,' Ian insisted to *Interview.* 'There's a consciousness in this country at the moment, a raising of the

intelligence. People are more aware of what's going on now, wanna know more, feel involved, more together. It's only ten years before the end of the century and changes are coming fast. Everyone's saying "What is it? What is it?" But it's in the air: you just can't say what it is.'

Within months however, he'd be slightly more reflective.

'I was in touch with my own spirit before,' Brown insisted to Nick Kent in *The Face,* 'so I don't believe E's changed me. But I can see it's changed a lot of other people. Only last year, people were taking it to extremes using it to dance themselves into a trance with.

Fook that. You've got to stay conscious, stay awake. Or else you're just like some old hippie. Right?'

Were the links between the Roses and E exaggerated?

'None of us were strung out at that time,' John Squire told me as I interviewed him for *I-D* in 1995. 'I can't remember my first E. Probably on tour somewhere when the band was breaking. Did it have a profound effect on me? If you go insane you've always gotta come back down. Ecstacy wasn't the band's fuel. That was a desire to succeed and create.'

And right now, The Stone Roses were burning up time.

## STORMING THE PALACE

AT the height of their success and at the zenith of their creative powers, the by now seemingly untouchable, immortal Stone Roses appeared at Alexandra Palace in North London on 9 November '89, their biggest 'happening' to date. Sold out weeks in advance it was intended as a glorious postscript to a remarkable year which had begun in front of 10 people in Hull. It wasn't a disaster but the event itself was far from well planned, being dogged by a succession of problems with poor acoustics, an inadequate PA and some horrendous organisation, which meant that a bar which could barely cope with 800 people struggled to deal with 8,000. Somewhere in the distance, John Squire was playing gloriously liquid, thrilling guitar runs. But there was no point. He was inaudible.

'They didn't seem to be conquering the logistics of playing a large gig,' commented Steve Sutherland in *MM*, 'let alone transcending the sum of their parts. It was OK as far as it went, which wasn't far enough, really.'

Ally Pally at least proved that The Stone Roses were human, something their most zealous, E-fuelled devotees had been inclined to forget. A few days later, they made a bizarre return to form. Appearing on BBC2's highbrow *The Late Show*, the band were 45 seconds into an incandescent 'Made Of Stone' when the fuses blew. The show's dumbstruck presenter, Tracy Macleod, rushed to the front of the stage to introduce the next item, while Ian Brown audibly ranted, 'Amateurs! Amateurs! We're wasting our time lads.'

It was a classic Roses moment, and meant that The Stone Roses could enter 1990 with high spirits and – always important for them, despite the public image – a bloody good laugh.

# Don't Stop

Glasgow Green, June 1990

**DON'T STOP**

AT the start of 1990 The Stone Roses were pictured – covered in snow, at the crest of a particularly spectacular, unknown high mountain. Up where they belonged, on top of the world.

Away from that glossy image, however, a few inevitable doubts were slowly starting to creep in.

'The bubble's bound to burst though, isn't it?' Ian Brown revealed uncharacteristic fears to *MM*. 'Name me one band that's lasted. The Rolling Stones? Pile of shit, man. That's not lasting is it? That's hanging on. They should put it out of its misery. We don't want to make idiots of ourselves like that. Basically, if we come out of this with no self respect then we've failed, man. It would mean nothing.'

In the same interview, the ever-thoughtful John Squire tackled the subject of pressure.

'Pressure?' he pondered. 'The only pressure we're under is the pressure we exert on ourselves. We've got our own standards to keep. The pressure is to make every record as good as the last one. To continually improve and to stop when we don't. Having the bottle to stop when we

■ an voices fears . . . trial by tabloid . . . splash 'n' grab raids . . . the Roses political hardline . . . Stone Roses arrested! . . . the press conference from Hell . . . 'One Love' disappoints . . . the Spike Island mega-rave . . . last gig for five years

'If we come out of this with no self respect, then we've failed'

## TRIAL BY TABLOID

FROM here on in, the Roses every movement would be subject to strict and probing tabloid analysis. The Roses were no longer by any stretch of the imagination an underground band, and were beginning to appreciate the various stresses, pressures and dubious 'responsibilities' that accompanied mainstream fame and its absurd expectations.

This process had begun shortly after the release of 'The Stone Roses', when *The Sun* and the rest of Fleet Street were desperate to sniff out the truth behind 'Elizabeth My Dear' – a harmless, post-'Scarborough Fair' lilting song that concerns itself with assassinating our beloved monarch.

*The Sun* spent weeks ringing up the band's associates and former girlfriends, digging around for a bit of dirt and finally turning up at Ian's mother's house, asking the neighbours what the singer's feelings towards the Queen were. 'It's his opinion,' they were gruffly rebuffed.

*The Daily Star* ran a supposed 'in-depth' report pointing out – as if we needed telling – that Ian Brown was his own man, not just the 'new Mick Jagger'. Finally, Tory MP Geoffrey Dickens seized on the band's perceived anti-Royalist sentiments as a way of making cheap political capital for himself.

'Ban these pop idiots,' screamed *The Star* after Dickens had tried to get the Roses banned from *Top Of The Pops* and, having failed, urged viewers to turn off in protest or phone the BBC to register a complaint.

Ian Brown was characteristically bemused.

'Trial by tabloid? That's OK,' he insisted to *Sounds.* 'We're already in the tabloids, last week. "Pop nutters The Stone Roses." It came from that *Sounds* interview a while ago where I fantasised about putting a blanket over the Queen Mother's head. Geoffrey Dickens was trying to get us banned from *Top Of the Pops* or get the viewers to switch off so the BBC wouldn't put us on again!

'That was our first tabloid press. the more the merrier. Front page every day. Forget The Sex Pistols, forget everybody. I want to see

realise we've lost it. Not to end up pimping ourselves. It happens to people without them realising it. Don't cater to an audience.'

In an untypical moment of public lucid insight, Ian Brown put things into some sort of perspective.

'We're not worried about anything,' insisted the singer with the Best, if not yet *quite* the Biggest Band On The Planet. 'Having a Top 40 hit isn't anything to worry about, is it? Worry is about having no money,

being hungry, having nowhere to live. Not being able to get a job when you want one. That's worry. Worry isn't doing your own thing and getting paid to do it, is it?'

Soon afterwards, interviewed by *Sounds,* Ian expressed untypical self-doubt.

'There's Stone Roses everywhere,' he decided. 'I can see why people get sick of it. People are bound to get tired of a group that are constantly in the press and on the radio.'

Funny thing is, they never did.

John told *Sounds*. 'You can't stick to your principles any more unless you've got a secret Swiss bank account to see you through once your funds have been sequestrated.'

But they didn't have all the answers.

'I don't know what the solution is,' Ian grumbled to *The Observer*. 'I just know there's a lot of people who stay on it, and that gives me inspiration. There's a bloke called Benny Rothman who led the Kinder trespass in the Thirties in the hills above Manchester where local people weren't allowed to go on the land. The first time he went on the land, all the lords whipped him to the ground. The next week he came back with 6,000 people and held firm, and that led to the setting up of the National Trust. And now he's having to organise it all again, because those lands have been bought by some Americans. Still there, at eighty. People like that you've got to listen to. Not people who scream and shout from the ages of fifteen till twenty-two and then stop.'

Now when was the last time you heard a quote like that from a so-called 'pop star'?

The Geoffrey Dickens incident also, obviously, brought the band's strong anti-Royalist beliefs into sharper focus, if indeed it were possible.

'I want Camelot to stop,' Ian had told me in my first interview with him, for my *Avanti!* fanzine in 1989. 'I always thought that if I was ever in a group I'd want to say that, and so I have on the LP. It's just an English person's observations about his England. There's no justification for the Royal Family anymore, never has been.'

'The Royal Family... the houses they live in have hundreds of rooms when half a mile down the road there's hundreds of people under a bridge,' Ian told *Sounds*. 'That's it. The Royal Family is a lynchpin of the English attitude, right down to whether you can get in a pub on a Saturday night with jeans on.'

Brown went much further in *Select*.

'What kind of country do we live in where people's movements are stopped by the police? Like in the miner's strike,' he quietly fumed. 'The poll tax riots? Inspired me.

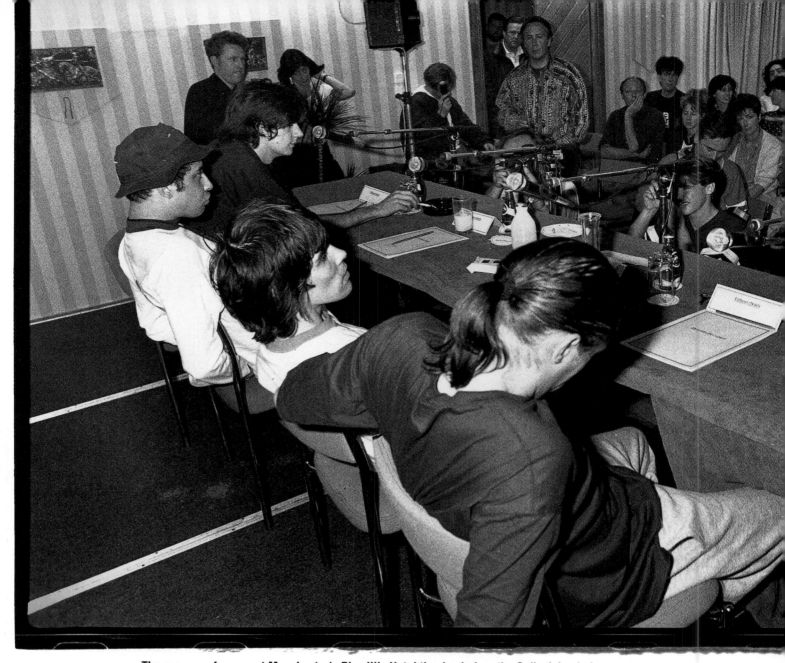

The press conference at Manchester's Picadilly Hotel the day before the Spike Island gig

Violence is the only way to achieve anything. The reason we're all in the position we are is because the people who have the power achieved it through violence.

'I'm ashamed to go abroad. People have got their ideas of what English people are like. I mean, we were the first country to set up concentration camps (during the Boer War). We stole land, shot children, shot women. People power as well comes through violence. Martin Luther King got shot, didn't he? Anyone who's brave enough to stand up against something if it's going to result in their own death. So be it. If you believe so strongly in what you're doing you should be prepared to die for it. Would I die for a cause? I would, yeah.'

Clearly, it looked like the Roses were heading for trouble, but when it came, it was from a source that nobody expected.

### PAINT SPLASH 'N' GRAB RAID

THE front page of the *Manchester Evening News* had it first, 'Stone Roses Held In Attack,' screamed the headlines on January 31. 'Pop Stars In £10,000 Raid Quiz.'

The Roses had been arrested!

On January 30, all four Stone Roses and their road manager Steve 'Adge' Atherton had driven up to Wolverhampton from Rockfield Studios in South Wales, where they were recording with John Leckie, to visit their former record company, FM Revolver. Angry at the label's re-release of their 1987 single 'Sally Cinnamon' – and specifically its accompanying video, they threw blue and white paint over label boss Paul Birch (35) and his girlfriend Olivia Darling (22). Ian Brown put a brick through Birch's £25,000 Mercedes.

Result: a long night in the cells and charges to follow.

Oh blimey!

'The video was insulting,' Brown said at the time. 'Blokes selling fruit, a few pigeons, some black woman holding a baby with the word 'world' over it, a picture of me on the front of *The Face,* a few people in flares... It

was insulting. So we went and painted 'im!'

The next day, the police arrived at Rockfield to interview the band, who still had traces of paint on their clothes. They were caught blue and white handed.

'If you'd have been there on the night you'd have seen why we f***in' did it,' raged Mani. 'Cos the guy was being a completely obnoxious character. He's making more money now than hes ever made before, out of us! And he's yelling "Make an appointment. Make an appointment." So we...

'Did him.

'But ten minutes after he's phoned the police he put out a press release to the papers, the music magazines, everyone. Cos his record was still just outside the 10 then. He was hoping to capitalise on it. That's the sort of tosser he is.'

Once again, the Roses strongly-held sense of justice had prevailed, although this time a very much stronger form of justice might have prevailed over them!

'Am I worried 'bout goin'. to jail?' an incredulous Reni gasped to *Select.* 'Course I am! Who wants to go to jail? Especially over a video!'

Luckily, the naughty bloomin' Roses were bailed, and, as John Squire was quick to admit, the publicity hadn't done them any harm. Immediately, the band issued a writ on Revolver to prevent them showing the 'Sally Cinnamon' video. Shortly afterwards, Silvertone's own re-releases of 'Elephant Stone' and 'Made Of Stone' went Top 10 and Top 20 respectively. The Stones Roses rollercoaster was still gathering pace.

On March 6, the Roses appeared at Wolverhampton Magistrates' Court charged with criminal damage. The case is adjourned when the defence and prosecution fail to agree on a figure for damage (the Roses reckon £8,000; the record company claim £22,000). The entire hearing lasted for 60 seconds, but it was far from the end of this particular story.

On March 31, the *NME* reported that Ian Brown was spotted at a London bar having an 'animated conversation' with the entire Liverpool football team. Reports also claimed that the Roses had pulled out of a proposed gig in Nimes, because it formed part of the local bullfighting season. 'The band don't want a ritual slaughter as a support act,' a spokesman said.

On May 14, *The Daily Mirror* reported 'Mayhem as stars are caught in a shoot out', describing how Ian, James' Tim Booth and other Roses were at a gig by reggae act Ini Kamoze at Gareth Evans' International Club when the roof was peppered by gunfire.

Thankfully, shortly afterwards, the band resumed something like normal service with a few gigs in Scandinavia. The first few were decidedly average, but the gig in Stockholm, attended by the *Melody Maker's* steadfastly loyal Bob Stanley, saw...

'The most impressive, exciting pop group in the world.'

James Brown, now editor of *Loaded,* was equally impressed, taking great care to note John's curious amalgam of floral shirt and combat trousers.

'Set alone, Squire's guitars could have strolled off some pre-punk golden rock album,' he beamed, 'rolling with the blues, stalked by Mani's bass, and crested with Reni's troubled funk drumming.'

Was this to be the future?

A few days later The Stone Roses were to play at their biggest happening yet: the gonzoid, monster, notorious Baggy Altamont, aka Spike Island.

But first...

## THE PRESS CONFERENCE FROM HELL

AT Manchester's Piccadilly Hotel on May 26, 1990, the day before Spike Island, a hundred members of the press, flown in specially from around the world, sat in a conference room. At one end there was a large table, four glasses of water and four microphones. The Stone Roses appeared from a side door to a smattering of applause and whistles. Then it all went wrong, the press conference ending in chaos as the band's aloof approach is slammed by journalists, who in turn are threatened by friends and fans of the band.

How come all *this* happened?

Here are a few excerpts from the Press conference from Hell. Mani: 'You can speak to us. Hello. Welcome to Manchester.' (No response.) Ian: 'Has anyone got any questions, or what?' Floor: 'Do you take a lot of drugs?' Ian: 'Do you take a lot of drugs? No. S'alright then innit.' Floor: 'Do you reckon your early demos are gonna be worth any money?'

Ian: 'They're worth about £2.50 now. Sell 'em.' Floor: 'Are you gonna do a full-scale tour of America or just a one-off date?' Ian: 'You'll never see us do a full scale tour. We're like cabbages most of the time.' (Long painful silence) Mani (impatiently): 'Come on, fire away.' Floor: 'Do you think you're the

Locally notorious friend of the Roses, Alphonso Buller

new Rolling Stones?' Ian: 'This is 1990 innit? So I say to you, the Rolling who?' It got worse. Floor: 'How do you think America is gonna appreciate Manchester sarcasm?' Ian: 'With an American accent, probably.' Floor: 'Since it's inevitable you guys are coming to America, you're obviously gonna have to do a lot of press. They'll want to ask you about your personal life, what are your backgrounds?' Ian: 'I'm not telling you.' (Five minutes silence and shuffling.) Madman grabbing microphone: 'WOOOOOOOOOAHHHHHHH! IN THE AREA!' (Another awkward silence). Ian (belches): 'Urgh. Scuse. Anyone want a cig.' And then things got even worse. Brown: 'Who's come from the other side of the world? Hands up, you're all being paid to ask questions.' (Angry rumblings.) Floor: 'I paid my own air fare, so f*** you, man!'

Ian: 'Ooooh.' (A row starts between two journalists. One of them turns on the Roses.) Angry bloke (former *MM* correspondent Frank Owen): 'This is f***ing bullshit. I'm from Manchester, I live in New York and this is bullshit. You're treating these people like f***ing shit.' (Another bloke starts telling him to shut up.) 'No, you shut up, you f***ing dickhead.' (They start pushing each other.) Ian: 'Hey, ease off, we're not treating anyone like anything.' Angry Worrall: 'Don't give me that, I'm from here. I know when you're winding people up!' Ian: Sort your head out, man.'

And even worse. (Everyone starts arguing and jostling with each other.) Member of band's entourage (picks up mike, shouting): 'How the f*** do you think the band feel sat up there in complete silence with all you bastards staring at them, asking them f*** all?! you come all this way, drink all the free beer and you haven't asked f***ing shit! You're a bunch of f***ing wankers, in whatever language you speak. If I was them I'd f*** off now.' (Whistling, shouting and shoving ensue. The band depart.)

Relations between the Roses and their press public had sunk to an extraordinary low.

Spike Island was next.

## ISLAND OF LOST SOULS

ON 27 May, 1990, The Stone Roses appeared before 28,000 (the official figure, but estimates had it nearer 40,000) on a mud flat near Widnes called Spike Island. The day of the concert, *The Daily Star* quoted Ian Brown as saying 'Margaret Thatcher should have gone up in the Brighton bomb' alongside the headline 'Acid Band Insult PM'.

Sadly, the gig wasn't quite as explosive. Again, like Ally Pally, organisational and sound problems dogged the event.

Everett True, writing in *Melody Maker*, declared:

'If Alexandra Palace was an ignominious failure, good intentions blown away on a sea of bad sound, Spike Island was even more so. The grander the scale, the harder they fall... But Spike Island was an event, and events, even if they are disasters at the time, are what count.'

Spike Island was meant to be this generation's Woodstock.

*Sounds* described 'A grassy knoll in the middle of the rusty, shitheap cement factory death belt of the Mersey... a very unlikely festival point.'

Still, at least only 27 people were hospitalised. There was one heart attack

Gareth Evans and Shaun Ryder – Spike Island

**Glasgow Green – the last Stone Roses gig for five years**

victim and only four arrests. Not bad statistics for such a massive event.

And *The Guardian* were fairly positive.

"Fools Gold', with probably the best helicopters, took off well but landed off-key. 28,000 fans and The Stone Roses failed to levitate Spike Island, but definitely kicked off the summer.'

More humorously, *NME* reported that 'One photographer looked at the stack of

amplifiers at either side of the stage and believed them to have been exactly the same as the ones used at The International in Manchester, the club owned by the band's manager, Gareth!'

Whatever did or did or did not happen at Spike Island, afterwards there was a tremendous, heavy feeling of disappointment, a feeling that more than just a gig had all gone badly wrong.

### IS THIS LOVE, OR CONFUSION?

FOUR days after the ill-fated concert, the Altamont of Baggy, *The Star* reported that the Roses were planning a 'secret' gig for 100,000 people outside Buckingham Palace. Another factually cobblers *Star* 'exclusive'! In June, various reports claimed that the artwork for the Roses' proposed next single, 'One Love', had been scrapped due to 'the suggestion of a swastika in John Squire's

How would we feel then? We didn't want it to get out of control. So we decided to nip it in the bud.'

It was as if the artwork fiasco had been a bad omen. 'One Love' – a loose, funky number along the lines of 'Fools Gold' – was generally poorly received, even as the single entered the chart at Number 4, the band's biggest hit to date.

'A dyslexic guitar drone,' complained *Melody Maker's* Jon Wilde (no fan of The Stone Roses).

*NME* made 'One Love' Single Of The Week, but an obvious display of sycophancy carried accompanying home truths.

'Initially a slight disappointment. There is something a bit inelegant about its structure. It sounds like it evolved from a very loose jam the band had one afternoon.'

Not quite saved by a typically honeyed chorus, 'One Love' wasn't a terrible Roses record, but it wasn't a great one either. It was a good record, which by their dizzying standards, wasn't good enough.

**Ian Brown and Peter Hook, backstage at Spike Island**

sleeve illustration.

'If you looked at it in a certain way it did look like a swastika in there,' a spokesperson admitted. 'As soon as John realised, he tore up the proofs.'

'You know, anyone who knows us knows we're not Nazis,' an irritated Ian told *Select.* 'But if some kid in Barcelona goes into a bar with a Stone Roses T-shirt on – looking a bit like a swastika – ends up getting stabbed.

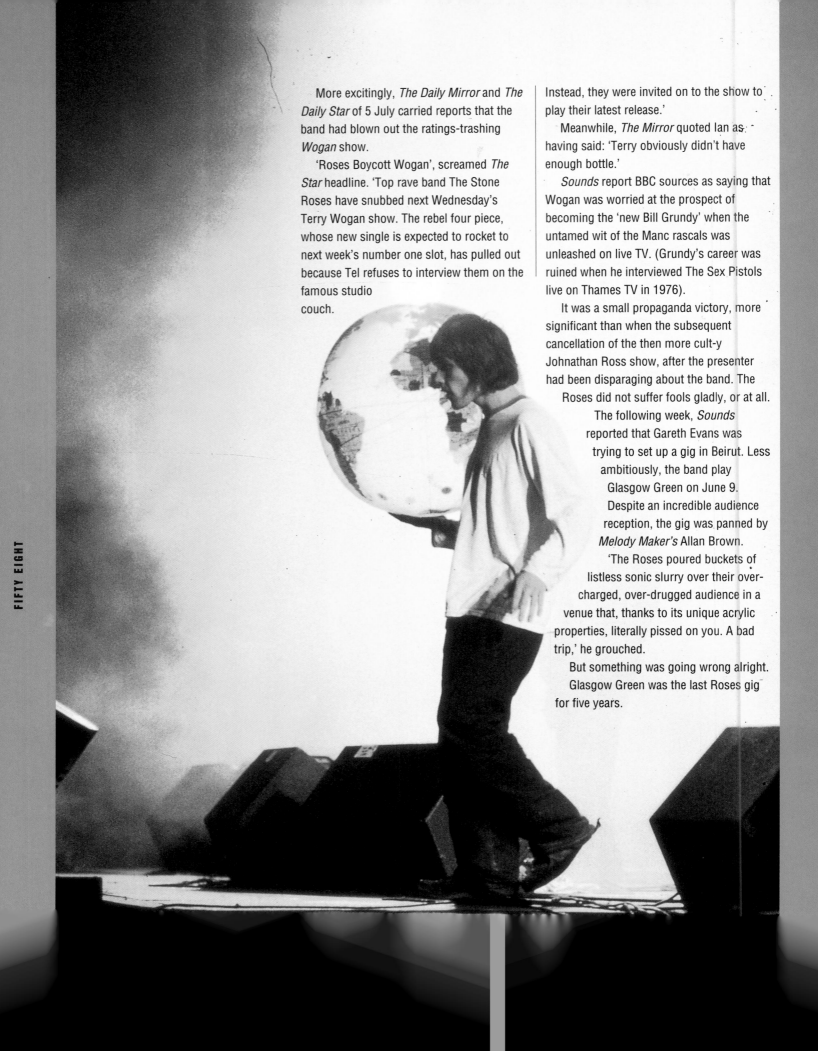

More excitingly, *The Daily Mirror* and *The Daily Star* of 5 July carried reports that the band had blown out the ratings-trashing *Wogan* show.

'Roses Boycott Wogan', screamed *The Star* headline. 'Top rave band The Stone Roses have snubbed next Wednesday's Terry Wogan show. The rebel four piece, whose new single is expected to rocket to next week's number one slot, has pulled out because Tel refuses to interview them on the famous studio couch.

Instead, they were invited on to the show to play their latest release.'

Meanwhile, *The Mirror* quoted Ian as having said: 'Terry obviously didn't have enough bottle.'

*Sounds* report BBC sources as saying that Wogan was worried at the prospect of becoming the 'new Bill Grundy' when the untamed wit of the Manc rascals was unleashed on live TV. (Grundy's career was ruined when he interviewed The Sex Pistols live on Thames TV in 1976).

It was a small propaganda victory, more significant than when the subsequent cancellation of the then more cult-y Johnathan Ross show, after the presenter had been disparaging about the band. The Roses did not suffer fools gladly, or at all.

The following week, *Sounds* reported that Gareth Evans was trying to set up a gig in Beirut. Less ambitiously, the band play Glasgow Green on June 9. Despite an incredible audience reception, the gig was panned by *Melody Maker's* Allan Brown.

'The Roses poured buckets of listless sonic slurry over their over-charged, over-drugged audience in a venue that, thanks to its unique acrylic properties, literally pissed on you. A bad trip,' he grouched.

But something was going wrong alright. Glasgow Green was the last Roses gig for five years.

# The Lost Years

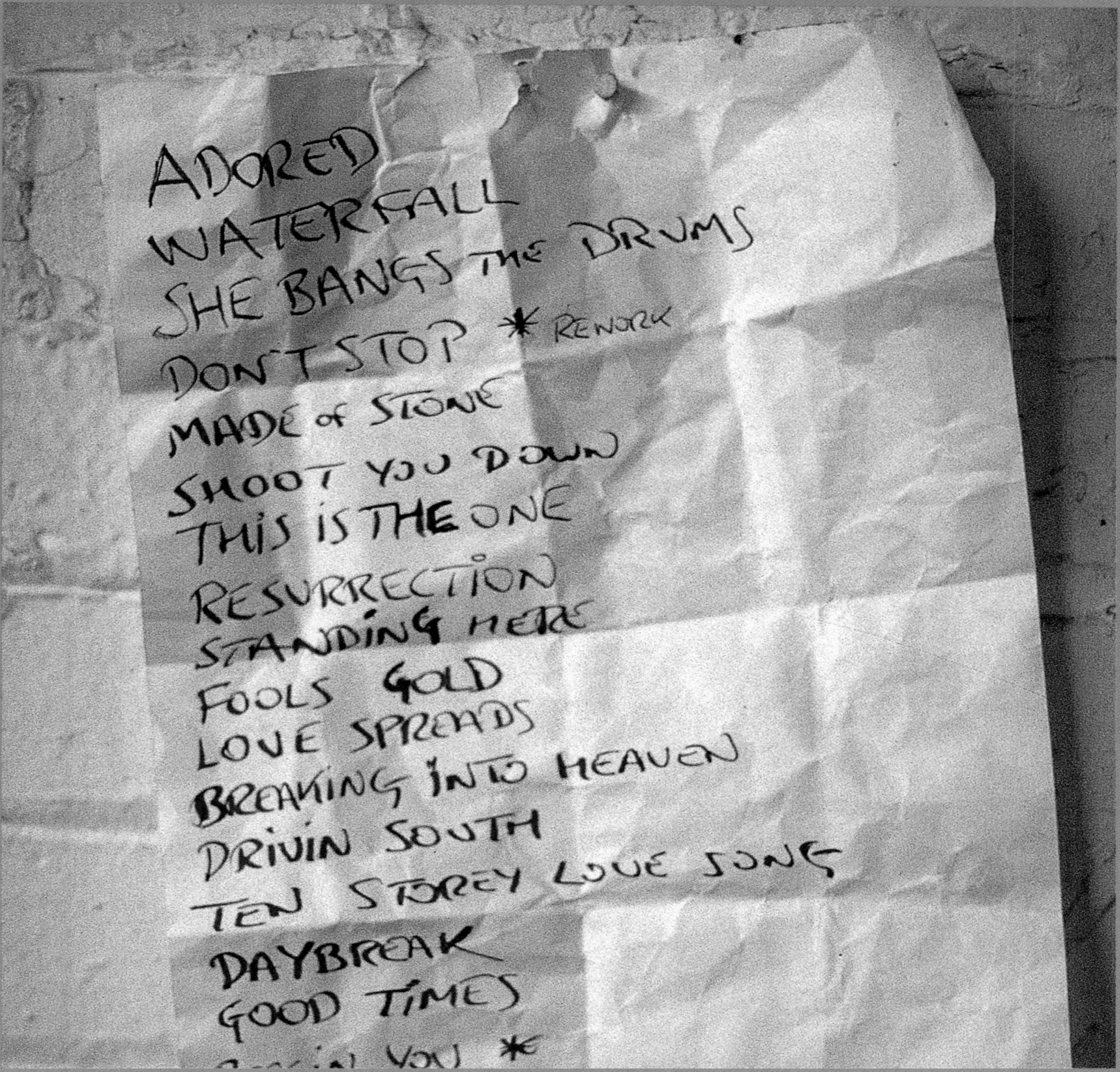

ADORED
WATERFALL
SHE BANGS THE DRUMS
DON'T STOP * REWORK
MADE OF STONE
SHOOT YOU DOWN
THIS IS THE ONE
RESURRECTION
STANDING HERE
FOOLS GOLD
LOVE SPREADS
BREAKING INTO HEAVEN
DRIVIN SOUTH
TEN STOREY LOVE SONG
DAYBREAK
GOOD TIMES
......... YOU *

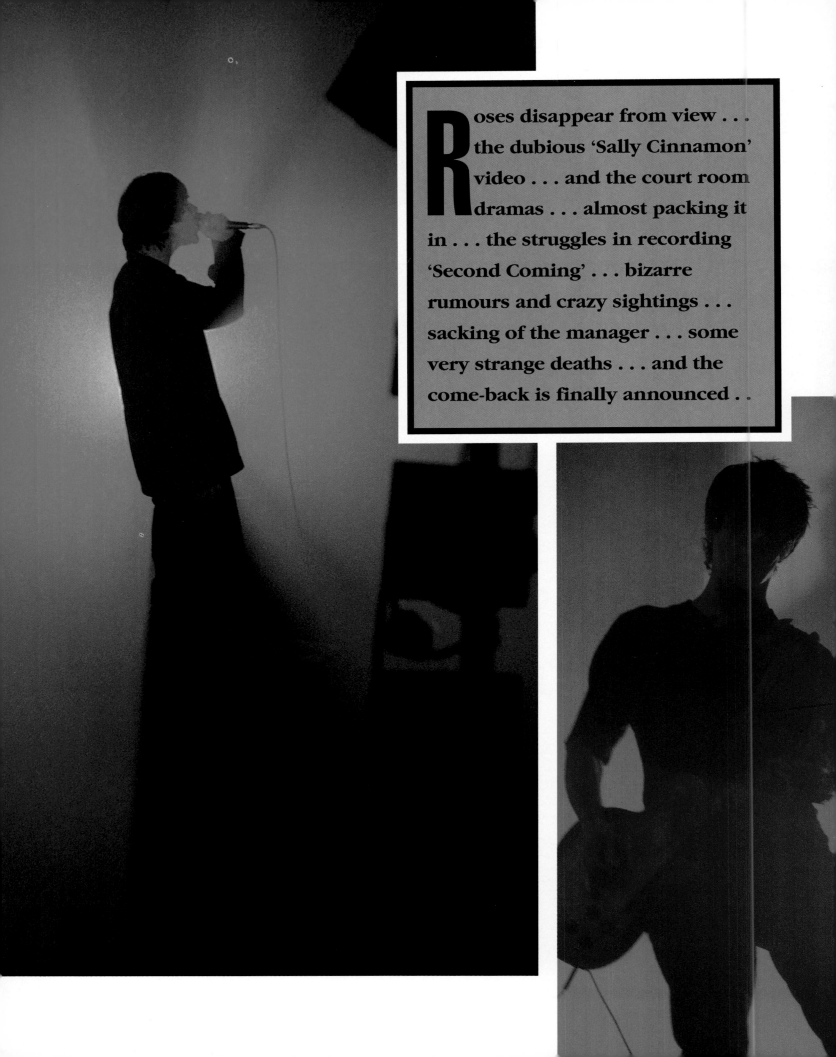

**R**oses disappear from view . . . the dubious 'Sally Cinnamon' video . . . and the court room dramas . . . almost packing it in . . . the struggles in recording 'Second Coming' . . . bizarre rumours and crazy sightings . . . sacking of the manager . . . some very strange deaths . . . and the come-back is finally announced . .

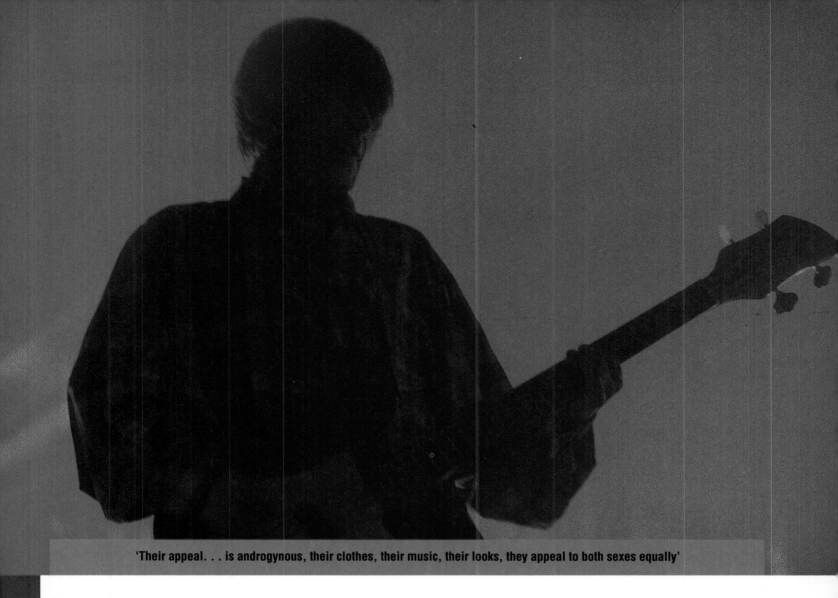

'Their appeal. . . is androgynous, their clothes, their music, their looks, they appeal to both sexes equally'

## WHERE IS THE PHUTURE?

TOWARDS the middle of '90, *MM's* Bob Stanley pondered the question – as posed by the popular Roses' fanzine 'Made Of Paper' – 'Where do we go from here?'

'I see The Stone Roses becoming the most successful band in the world,' insisted Bob, before adding, 'How can such a cosmic claim be backed up?

'Well, their appeal – as with all the great pop icons from Elvis to Prince – is androgynous, their clothes, their music, their looks, they appeal to both sexes equally. This appeal is universal. Happy Mondays, by comparison, are basically a lads band and could only appeal to girls as dirty sex. Secondly, they cut across pop, dance and rock, the three major musics of today, picking up fans in all sectors with consummate ease. The only enemies they seem to have encountered en route are old

heads either too scared or too cynical to come to terms with the new order. The third and least tangible point, they have a magical knack for doing The Right Thing. When they say they're going to be huge in America you believe them, don't doubt them for a minute. Happy Mondays, the only group who could conceivably challenge them, may have the loon reputation, but their recent career has been carefully managed, and their rise from Dingwalls to Town & Country Club to Wembley Arena is a flawless computer printout for a successful rock group. Soon they will slog around America believing you have to before you become accepted there. The Stone Roses will turn up, expect adulation, and receive it. It's that untogether and that perfect.'

At the time, Bob's analysis seemed bang on. With hindsight, the word 'untogether' seems more accurate than 'perfect'. The first

sign of trouble came in midsummer, when the Roses unceremoniously blew out their entire American tour, squandering all the interest generated by Stateside radio play.

'America doesn't deserve us yet,' gushed Ian, immodest as ever.

'We're just naturally stubborn,' muttered John to *Select.* 'If we get pressurised into going to America, which we have been, we'll turn it down.'

But there was more to it than that. As *MM* wrote of the Roses' being 'crucified by their own Messiah complex' and of 'a peculiar death wish' taking over the band, rumblings had it that the Roses were becoming extremely dissatisfied with their Silvertone eight album recording contract. Finally, on September 15, *MM* reported that the Roses were trying to leave the label. In response, Silvertone slapped an injunction on the band, preventing them from recording

**The Roses hit the headlines in paint fiasco**

for any other company. The band claimed their contract was 'restrictive'. Over the next few years, the band would spend as much time in a courtroom as they would in a recording studio.

### THEY FOUGHT THE LAW (1)

BEFORE the Silvertone hearing, the band were due back in court over the good old paint splattering fiasco. On October 9, 1990, all four Roses traipsed into Wolverhampton Crown Court to be described as 'four young men with an obsessive regard for their music' and duly fined £3,000 each.

In defence, their own brief described the band as 'stupid', but added 'They believed the release (of 'Sally Cinnamon' and the dubious promo vid) to be damaging to their professional reputation, so decided to take the law into their own hands.

'These four young men are not merely fussy,' he explained, 'but obsessive about the quality of everything associated with their name. They want to be the best at what they do and they are never satisfied with

second best. It is a genuine desire on their part that their fans should not be ripped off.'

Outside the courtroom, fans wore T-shirts proclaiming 'The Manchester Four Are Innocent', while the judge, in his summing up, described the band as 'immature to the point of childishness', adding that 'a prison sentence might otherwise lead to notoriety, and I certainly don't want to be responsible for that'!

The story made all the tabloids. *Q* reported a passing roadie commenting, 'It might not be a bad idea to send them down. At least they might get on and write some new songs.'

Meanwhile, *Sounds* claimed Ian Brown had been overheard saying that he always wanted to be in a band that became really massive and then never did anything again!

As the nation gasped, the story was denied.

### THEY FOUGHT THE LAW (2)

THE Silvertone case came to court in March 1991, where some weeks later, presiding

Judge Humphries declared the Silvertone contract 'entirely one-sided and unfair.'

Following the verdict, the Roses signed to Geffen for a reported advance of four million pounds, a deal which insiders reckoned could eventually net the band upwards of twenty million. If they'd have lost the court case, John reckoned they'd have gone back on the dole and issued bootlegs!

### THEY FOUGHT THE LAW (3!)

MEANWHILE, during the various cases, the Roses had become unhappy with some of manager Gareth Evans' showbizness tactics. Why, for example, had he allowed them to be signed to the prohibitive Silvertone deal? Other rumblings concerned the size of Mr. Evans' cut of the Roses' finances, royalties from Tshirt sales etc. etc. Maybe they'd been just a little naive.

'Gareth's an obsessive,' Ian told *Sounds* in '89. 'He's on our side – we can't be arsed with all that business stuff.'

Whatever, in February '92, the Roses fired Gareth Evans. Three years later, Evans filed a ten million quid lawsuit alleging wrongful dismissal. Finally, the case was settled out of court, the band considering it a victory.

'The Roses have always had a sense of justice and they feel vindicated by the result,' quipped a spokesperson.

Right. But where was the music?

## THE LORD LUCANS OF POP
NOWHERE, that's where.

'If it's a case of hard gigging over the next five years, I think they'd rather stay in bed,' – Andrew Lauder, Silvertone Records, 1990.

In June '91, *MM* reported that the band were looking at studios and that an album would be out by the end of the year. Nothing happened. In July, the Roses were reputed to be in Cornwall with John Leckie, producer of that gold dust-spangled debut album, now seemingly light years ago. Nothing happened. The band were then meant to be

recording in Wales, using The Rolling Stones' mobile. Again, nothing happened. The only news around this time was then Reni was to appear in court in Manchester over a charge of obstructing police, relating to a parking incident in August. He was fined £50 and, we hoped, told to get on with playing drums, not playing hooky.

Subsequently, a bizarre form of rumour mill began to establish itself regarding the Roses. Some of the rumours were just too ridiculous to be believed. Or were they? The band had become heroin addicts!?! The band had become *golf* addicts!?!!! The band had hired a fleet of Ford Fiestas and could be seen hurtling around the Welsh countryside. Other stories seemed to contain a mixture of malice, hearsay and disposable halftruths. According to one gossip, Ian Brown was reportedly eighteen stone!

Meanwhile, the group were recording with

a succession of producers. In January '95, *FHM* described a 1993 recording session with John Leckie thus:

'The band apparently spent most of the day in bed, would get up, smoke about an ounce of weed, get the £250-a-day programming guy to loop up a beat from a King Tubby record and then decide they didn't like it.'

During this period, Ian Brown signed a rehearsal room book as 'The laziest man in show business'!

In July '93, John Leckie finally quit, to be replaced by former engineer Paul Schroeder and, later, Rockfield Studio tapes man, Simon Dawson. On his exit, John Leckie revealed 'In a way we spent two years looking for a new sound, and then came back to where we started.'

At the end of the year, the band asked close friend and publicist Philip Hall to

**'It's a fair cop!' – Glasgow Green**

manage them. He agreed, but within weeks tragically died of cancer. The band attended the funeral. Philip's widow, Terri, took over the group's publicity, thus ensuring the tight inner circle remained. (In a bizarre twist, in '95 the Roses asked former Led Zeppelin manager Peter Grant to handle their affairs. He refused, and he too would be dead within a few months.)

Meanwhile, the band set about spending some of their recording advance on houses for their parents, and starting their own families. Between times, musical empires tumbled. Baggy was now hopelessly derided, the result of Happy Mondays' orgiastic split (in '92) and too many pale Roses/Mondays imitations, such as The Soup Dragons. Nirvana became massive, reintroduced guitar rawk, and Kurt Cobain killed himself. Dance became huge in the mainstream, and then subsided. Later, Britpop emerged, with scene-stealers Oasis (whose singer Liam Gallagher owned no less than *four* copies of 'The Stone Roses') claiming direct inspiration from the Mancunian candidates. Who were – of course – still nowhere to be seen.

Perhaps The Stone Roses were work shy, but there was also the not-so-small matter of the massive expectations which would greet

a new record. After all, how do you follow complete perfection?

Eventually, rumours of a new album surfaced in late 1994; not a moment too soon! 'It's gonna be the full-on Led Zeppelin,' excitedly claimed one news item. 'They're gonna blow everybody's minds,' raved another.

This time, the stories were true after all . The Stone Roses were coming back.

**Workshy? Mani sits this one out**

Ian – 'The laziest man in show business'

Reni at the conga drums

★★★★★★★★★★★★★★★★★

# Resurrection
# and Reshuffle

### LOVE RESURRECTION

ON November 7, 1994, the Roses' comeback single made its first appearance on Steve Lamacq's Radio One show. The song unveiled a new Stone Roses. Gone were the honeyed, almost Sixties derived melodies and Eighties funk undercurrents of their last incarnation. 'Love Spreads' boasted a typically sly Roses lyric (about the patriarchal Christian tradition) and a looser, harder rock sound. It was, as many people noted, the spiritual descendant of Led Zeppelin's 'Moby Dick'. But from John Squire's dazzling, heartfelt guitar playing to Ian's nasal vocals, it was still – most definitely – *the Roses.*

Happily, the single was almost universally well received.

'They used to mix their songs backwards, now John Squire's guitar sound itself has been sucked back through time,' I raved in *MM.* 'The Roses have taken on rock and emerged with their dignity intact.'

*NME's* editor, Steve Sutherland, declared 'Clever. Instead of trying to move with the times, the Roses have relaxed and let the times move back around them. 'Love

**T**he Roses return with 'Love Spreads' . . . differing reactions to the 'Second Coming' album . . . John falls ill . . . Reni leaves! . . . the first live gig for five years . . . John smashes his collarbone and the Roses cancel Glastonbury . . . the rows are revealed . . . live triumphs in Britain . . . John announces his decision to quit !! . . .

Be Your Fantasy', with fans in some cities reporting difficulties in finding the record in the shops. Were the Roses' cursed?

Still, if 'Love Spreads' unveiled a new, rockier Roses sound, the band themselves seemed unchanged. In typical fashion, they turned down *Top Of The Pops,* and managed to alienate large sections of the music press by granting the sole interview to promote their return to *The Big Issue,* the magazine set up to aid the homeless. It was a typical Roses gesture, and the interview itself was typically unrevealing. No change there.

Then, on December 5, an album. The brilliantly, boldly, irrepressibly Roses titled 'Second Coming' hit the streets after a tight security campaign had prevented any copies falling into the hands of nasty reviewers. In London and Manchester, expectant fans queued up outside record stores for hours, eager to get their hands on this five years-in-the-waiting arty-fact.

When 'Second Coming' hit the turntables, it was obvious that the Led Zeppelin-chomping rock beast of 'Love Spreads' was no one-off. The album was almost unrecognisable from the Roses' debut. Sure,

**John in the 'Love Spreads' video, Los Angeles January '95**

some grooves remained, notably the semi-Techno monster rock of 'Begging You', but they were darker, more like the grindings of huge machinery rather than nimble funk workouts. John Squire's guitar playing almost dominated the album and had undergone a remarkable transition, into deathshead blues, heartbreaking axe howls, and bloodied swamp-rock. Then there were the lyrics. Familiar themes of justice and love/hate cropped up on songs like 'How Do You Sleep?', one of their finest ever moments, pure rapture. But songs such as 'Good Times' and 'Tightrope' were awash with images of upheaval, betrayal, breakdown and death.

Whatever had happened to the Roses in the last five years, it didn't sound like – pardon the pun – a bed of roses.

'Second Coming' confused, thrilled and divided equally.

For *Select,* it was 'a great record. Loose, funky, paranoid, enough echoes of the debut to remind you why you loved them first time around, and bold enough to compare with the best they've done.'

*Time Out* however were less convinced: 'A relatively pleasing but far from breathtaking work.'

*Vox* were undecided, being more impressed with John Squire's contributions than the album as a whole: 'Squire's mercurial energy and tireless invention contrast sharply with the rest of the group.'

*Q* were almost appalled: 'As often as they hit the much-publicised Led Zeppelin button, they hit the ones marked Humble Pie and Robin Trower. 'Second Coming' is just OK, which in itself is a disappointment.'

*NME* (perhaps still smarting from the *Big Issue* snub) were damning: 'Anti-climax blues band'.

*The Face, The Guardian* and *The Daily Telegraph* were full of guarded praise.

But *Melody Maker* were truly exultant: 'The five- year delay is worth it... Ian Brown has rarely sounded so f***-me-dead beautiful, all graceful and relaxed, sympathetic and tender... Mr. Squire's guitar breaking out in spasmodically funkdafied spots all over, Reni's percussion as natural and flowing as you'd wish. F***. This is the resurrection, indeed.'

Indeed. Still, some reviewers grumbled at the five years taken by the Roses to make 'Second Coming', when in fact the Roses debut LP had also, effectively, drawn on five years of experience.

Remember the doubters first time around? Whatever the mixed critical viewpoint, 'Second Coming' entered the BBC charts at Number Four (Number One in MRIB's), and has since gone platinum, selling 300,000 copies. How ever you may look at it, this is definitely not at all bad for a supposed 'anticlimax'!

The next step was to do it live.

**Midnight at the HMV store, Market Street, Manchester as fans queue for 'Second Coming'**

## COMEBACK IN LANGUOR

ON 28 January 1995, *Melody Maker* announced the Roses plans for a string of secret UK dates in March, when more would be revealed about their new gonzo rock direction and whether they could – after a five year absence – cut it as a live act. Then, suddenly, a sizable spanner was thrown into the works with the shock announcement, on February 25, that John Squire was seriously ill. Strangely, differing reports alleged 'pneumonia' or 'pleurisy', depending on what paper you read. And then, to confuse matters further, reports from America revealed that John had confessed to a cocaine problem during the making of 'Second Coming'.

'I made the mistake of using cocaine for a while,' the genius guitarist was reported to have told the *LA Times*, 'thinking it would make me more productive. But it just made me more unsure, more paranoid.'

What *was* going on?

Whatever the truth of the John Squire illness, the resurrected (pending doctors' reports!) Roses released the second single from 'Second Coming', 'Ten Storey Love Song', on February 27. The song was top drawer, immortal Roses, a melody line to break most hearts coupled with one of Ian's most rousing, lovelorn vocals.

'An undeniable gem,' was the enthusiastic response from *Smash Hits.*

'Guitar licks that could send the sparrows crashing down from heaven,' raved *MM's* Everett True. "Ten Storey Love Song' is a classic old-style Roses ballad, guaranteed to bring a shiver to the vertebrae of even the most self-consciously contemporary of critics.'

It sold well too, cruising effortlessly into the Top Five. At the same time, the American release of 'Second Coming' hit Number 47 on the *Billboard* chart, a massive achievement for a group that had never

played live in America. Promoting the record in the US, Ian Brown caused howls of outrage and jammed switchboards after he appeared on a Los Angeles radio station and

**John recovers from double pneumonia in Los Angeles**

told the American Army in no uncertain terms to 'Stop killing babies.'

The same old Ian.

John's illness and the fact that the dates were no longer secret meant the cancellation of the proposed UK tour. In another weird twist, the band announced the severance of their partnership with former Guns 'N' Roses manager Doug Goldstein, with whom they'd been working for three months. Once again, The Stone Roses were unmanaged. But it was now established that they'd at last make their much trumpeted live return on April 19, at Oslo's Rockerfella club, tour managed – as in the old days – by Steve 'Adge' Atherton, who Ian met during the early warehouse days when 'Adge' stepped in to prevent a fight.

## WHO BANGS THE DRUMS?

ON 4 April '95, yet another bombshell emerged from the Roses' camp: drummer Reni had quit the group! Sadly, it was all true: the man whose unfeasibly funky skin-bashings had illuminated two albums was no longer a Stone Rose.

*MM* reported:

'The reasons for the split remain

shrouded in mystery, with some sources blaming his 'unreliable behaviour' and others claiming it relates to a dispute over publishing royalties. Reni failed to turn up for a number of press and publicity photo sessions this year, and the Roses even shot the video for 'Ten Storey Love Song' without him when he couldn't be located.'

Mystery remained.

**Reni in LA (left) and (above) his successor Robbie Maddix**

Equally worryingly, in an *NME* interview in March, John Squire said: 'We hope we will be together this time next year, but we can't say... it's a random universe. I can really see us all drifting apart if the band didn't exist.'

Subsequently, rumours surfaced of rows during the recording of 'Second Coming'. Again, a mystery. What *was* certain was that Reni's replacement was to be Robbie Jay Maddix, a 25-year-old from Manchester who'd previously worked with Terence Trent D'Arby and The Rebel MC.

No Reni?!! Could The Stone Roses ever be the same again?

The answer came on 19 April. No, the Roses could not be the *same* again, but yes, they could still be an earth-shattering live proposition.

'They launch into 'Ten Storey Love Song' and the ante is upped,' I raved of the gig in Oslo, at a rundown 2000-capacity venue in the middle of the red light district. 'You can feel the years melting away. Behind John Squire, four Fender Twins emphasise the shift from the old Roses into a harder, more guitar-frenzied, rock-smokin' beast.'

Mid-set, I remember just standing, silent, towards the back of it all, thrilled by the tug of the Roses' sweet sound and the enormity of the situation.

Prior to the gig, the Roses seemed surprisingly relaxed, Mani emphasising their embrace of rock history by strumming chords to 'Love's Alone Again' during the soundcheck. Afterwards, the band were penned in their dressing room for over an

**Robbie in full swing at Brixton Academy, December '95**

'Genius and madness are a thin line, man,' snapped Mani. 'Ask him if you want to know anything about it.'

Shortly afterwards, I brought up the thorny subject of rumours circulating in the music industry that the reason Reni left was down to heroin.

'That's a bit snide, man,' insisted Mani, reasonably enough. 'Reni's made a decision and it's bullshit to even speculate. It's nobody's business but his, man.'

Then I chatted to Robbie Maddix, the new drummer. He seemed an up character, someone who the Roses could probably use being around.

## SECOND COME, SECOND BEST?

In the same *MM* interview, I commented that while I thought 'Second Coming' was a brilliant album, better than Oasis' debut, it must have rankled that the other, increasingly huge Mancunian band had stolen the Roses' commercial thunder.

Mani was unfazed.

'Oasis are doin' their thing. F***in' like 'em, mate,' he urged. 'They're the most exciting thing that's happened to English music in years. F*** everyone else, they really mean it.'

'I don't see that there's any competition,' said Ian. 'It ain't the Premier League. If someone says to me they've started a band cos of seein' mine, and they're good, then I'm pleased about it. When Oasis started to come through who did they 'ave? Who was the competition?'

Mani, too, was unimpressed with the British music scene that greeted the Roses' return, a theme he'd return to in interviews throughout the year.

'The British music scene is as stale as it's ever been,' he ranted. 'The only stuff that interests me is the stuff I hear in clubs, or the Tricky LP. Music in Britain is wandering aimlessly about with medium length brown hair and a side parting. No f***er's shakin' it up, are they? Oasis wipe the floor with Blur, Pulp, all them f***ers man. Cos they mean it.'

For the Roses, 'meaning it' has always meant everything.

---

hour by awestruck Norwegian fans. Then, to my utmost surprise, they agreed to give a full, in-depth interview.

We talked about fans, the Roses' own mistrust of hero worship, politics, lyrics, the mixed reception to 'Second Coming', playing live, Kurt Cobain, John's reported 'coke problem'... All sorts of stuff.

But first, obviously, I asked about Reni.

'Time ran its course,' said Ian, painfully slowly. 'The way it is is the way it is. He'd had enough so he left.'

Ian Brown stared directly at the floor.

'Over the years we've often talked about leaving but we've been mates, buds, for twelve years.'

'Reni's been talking about leaving for about a year,' revealed John.

I mentioned Reni's 'unreliability'. Mani suddenly became irritated.

'We can't diss him, man,' he snapped. 'Reni's had a lot of bad shit in his life and... You get onto something else, man. You ain't gonna get shit out of us.'

I commented that Reni was something of a 'percussive genius'.

I COMMENTED on the underlying themes of 'Second Coming', and the lyrical sense of doom and despondency that hangs over it.

Was the album the diary of a crack-up?

'There is a lot of nihilism,' agreed Mani.

I was thinking of songs such as 'Good Times', 'Tears' in particular: '*Trapped in a maze of my own making/I'm going down...*'

'I had a bad day when I wrote 'Tears',' muttered John.

He didn't care to expand on it. Then, suddenly and unprompted, Mani said something highly revealing.

''Good Times' is just a focus on what's happenin', he said. 'Everyone's on smack. F***in' up. I've had 15 of my friends die in the last year cos of heroin. Another one went last week, methadone. It's a scourge, man. A f***in' waste. People get into it cos they've got f*** all to do, man. They've got twenty-four hours a day to kill, man.'

'It's a hobby,' added John.

Yeah, whatever had been going on in the five years prior to 'Second Coming', it most certainly had not been a bed of roses.

## HOT UNDER THE COLLAR

THE Roses continued touring around Europe, where reports of gigs ranged from the ecstatic (Madrid) to their disastrous (Copenhagen). The band were due to headline June's Glastonbury Festival, a massive return which should have proved the highlight of their career. Then disaster struck. On June 2 1995, following a string of US dates, John Squire smashed his collarbone in a cycling accident in San Francisco. The Roses' would not be appearing at Glastonbury. Their place was taken by Pulp, who triumphed at the festival.

1995 was rapidly turning into a particularly thorny year.

'We keep getting knocked back,' a worried Ian Brown told *Q*.

'The first thing I felt I was gutted,' he expanded in *MM*. 'We were leaving for Japan at half-eight in the morning. At half-five I got a phone call. It was Robbie saying, 'Is your bags packed?' I said, 'Yeah.' He said, 'You ain't going nowhere, we're going home, he's come off his bike.'

'I though, "Oh shit". It didn't really hit me 'til we got back to England and we sat and had breakfast in London airport. And we just looked at each other and said, "Oh no."'

Was there to be no end to the setbacks? Furthermore, many observers cast doubt upon the accident.

'People don't believe the Roses anymore,' sniped *NME*.

Poor John – lying injured in a San Francisco hospital – must have been feeling even worse!

**December 1994, and Reni is conspicuous by his absence**

carry the band beyond small career hiccups like not releasing an album for five years.'.

Ho ho. But things were looking up. Subsequently, John Squire designed a sleeve for 'War Child' and mixed a live version of 'Love Spreads' for the 'Help' Bosnia charity album. For The Stone Roses, charity never began at home.

In October, Ian lost two teeth following an attack in a Tokyo nightclub, suffering problems with his voice on a subsequent Australian tour.

Britain – at last – was next. A couple of days before the December '95 tour, I found John Squire in strangely reflective mood. We talked about the darkness of 'Second Coming', a brilliant antithesis to the beery cheeriness of Britpop.

'I listened to myself a lot, and Led Zeppelin, but not exclusively, whilst recording,' John revealed. 'We just plug away. If we do cross paths with popular culture then it's by accident. That's what happened last time.'

And what of the mood of the album?

'It wasn't a happy time,' murmured the guitarist. 'Can I detach myself playing those songs live? Mostly. But occasionally one will

stick a knife in. You can get a bit sensitive.'

Did the Roses feel different now from 1989/'90?

'I feel different,' considered John. 'There are times onstage when I look at Mani and think 'I wish we both felt like this five years ago, I feel more like we belong, in pop music that is. Less like interlopers'

Naturally, I asked John about the 'coke problem'.

'I'm not a party animal,' he said. 'The only reason it came up was cos I told a journalist in LA that part of the reason the album took so long was cos...

He paused.

'There were too many drugs in the studio. It can be destructive if everybody's on a different plane.'

Was that what happened?!

'A lot of the time, yeah. Who was on what? I don't wanna play the grass. It was a fractious time.'

What were the disagreements?

'Er, attendance at the studio, and... Who was the main culprit? You're turning this into a tale-telling session.'

It was just interesting that 'Second Coming' is very much a John Squire album.

## FLOWERS GROW AGAIN

AT last, bright spots appeared on the horizon. In July, the Roses' projected UK tour sold out 19 venues – 45,000 tickets in 24 hours. Then, on August 6, the Roses (bolstered by the addition of keyboard player/backing vocalists Nigel Ipinson and with John held together by steel pins!) headlined Feile Festival in Ireland, to good reviews, including a surprising rave notice in *NME.* Shortly afterwards, the band performed a secret gig at Pilkington, by way of a 'thank you' to Glastonbury organiser Michael Eavis. Robin Denselow of *The Guardian* was there, and reported:

'Immense, passionate workouts from the quiveringly appropriate 'I Am The Resurrection' to the monster rock of 'Love Spreads' were wielded with an authority that

**Mani chills – Brixton Academy 1995**

Cambridge 1995, and Ian surveys the crowd

John was the one who usually got things going, then?

'Yeah... well, I dunno. The stuff I was doing was *tangible.*'

Again I asked about Reni.

John fell silent, then said this: 'I think you either feel like you belong, or you don't. He couldn't have felt like he belonged. He wasn't turning up for things. I was annoyed when he left, yeah, cos you're only as strong as your weakest link. But what could we do about it? There's not really much you can do with a grown man.'

Throughout the conversation, John Squire seemed like a man carrying a burden. He told me things about his personal situation – private things, which I needn't reveal – and added that the band seemed to be suffering communication breakdowns.

'We talk a lot less,' John said.

John Squire admitted that the group became less close during the making of 'Second Coming' and that he and Ian have attempted songwriting on the road but 'nothing came of it.' He didn't know who his closest friend is these days. It wasn't Ian.

It was hard not to feel concern for the sensitive, gifted guitarist.

What was the happiest John Squire has ever been?

'Probably some seemingly insignificant moment,' he decided. 'Reading the paper in the sunshine outside, a particularly good bottle of beer. And you'll think "This is very pleasant." And it'll last for a few seconds and because you've studied it, it'll evaporate. Fleeting glimpses like that.

'I worry after every song that I'll forget how to do it,' he told me. 'There's still so much music left to come. I intend to grow bald and grey in public. Yeah, hopefully in this band.'

### GIFTS FROM A ROSE

TWO days later, The Stone Roses returned to a live triumph. The U.K. tour was everything it promised to be and more, with most gigs provoking rapturous, hysterical scenes among a fan base that had waited five years to see their favourites.

'As 'I Am The Resurrection' turns encore into revelation, The Stone Roses sound perilously close to being the most vital, essential rock band on the planet', gleefully slobbered *NME.*

At the end of the year, the new Roses played two enormous gigs – one at Sheffield Arena with former Happy Mondays mucker Shaun Ryder, back with new group Black Grape, the other at Wembley Arena, supported by Manic Street Preachers. Again, the gigs were triumphant.

'The Unforgettable Squire', declared the *NME* headline.

'Tonight, The Stone Roses brought the rusty angels down from caroling on high and set their wings ablaze,' raved *Melody Maker's* Everett True.

Up where they belonged, again.

## EPILOGUE

ON APRIL 1, 1996, Roses PR Terri Hall released the following statements:

(1) 'The following is a statement from The Stone Roses about John Squire's recent departure from the band. The news broke at the end of last week and was confirmed on Radio One's *Evening Session* on Monday 25 March. The band will not be available for any further comment on the subject and I would ask that you respect their feelings at this time. Thank you.

'We feel as cheated as everyone else who's heard the news. We are now in the middle of recording the next LP. We're disgusted, yet feeling stronger and more optimistic than ever.

Ian Brown, Mani, Robbie Maddix and Nigel Ipinson, 28 March 1996.'

(2) 'After lengthy deliberation, it is with great regret that I feel compelled to announce my decision to leave The Stone Roses. I believe all concerned will benefit from a parting of the ways at this point, and I see this as the inevitable conclusion to the gradual social and musical separation we've undergone in the last few years.

'I wish them every success and hope they go on to greater things. My intentions are to continue writing whilst looking for partners in a new band, and to begin working again as soon as possible. Thanks for everything.

John Squire April 1 1996.'

What now?

Perhaps the story of The Stone Roses is a tragedy, of a band who had it all and – as John put it to me – 'lost their impetus.'

Then again, perhaps the story of the Roses is one of triumph: of a band who overcame seemingly insurmountable difficulties to scale the peaks of pop. Not once, but twice, and arguably three times.

The Stone Roses: 'The Best Band On The Planet'. And you can't get better than that.